D1117748

VALUATION
WORKBOOK

WITHDRAWN

WINNETKA-NORTHFIELD
PUBLIC LIBRARY DISTRICT
WINNETKA, IL
446-7220

Founded in 1807, John Wiley & Sons is the oldest independent publishing company in the United States. With offices in North America, Europe, Australia and Asia, Wiley is globally committed to developing and marketing print and electronic products and services for our customers' professional and personal knowledge and understanding.

The Wiley Finance series contains books written specifically for finance and investment professionals as well as sophisticated individual investors and their financial advisors. Book topics range from portfolio management to e-commerce, risk management, financial engineering, valuation and financial instrument analysis, as well as much more.

For a list of available titles, visit our web site at www.WileyFinance.com.

VALUATION WORKBOOK

STEP-BY-STEP EXERCISES AND TESTS TO HELP YOU MASTER *VALUATION*

FOURTH EDITION

McKinsey & Company, Inc.

Tim Koller

Marc Goedhart

David Wessels

Jeffrey P. Lessard

WILEY

JOHN WILEY & SONS, INC.

This book is printed on acid-free paper. ∞

Copyright © 1990, 1994, 2000, 2006 by McKinsey & Company, Inc. All rights reserved.

Published by John Wiley & Sons, Inc., Hoboken, New Jersey.
Published simultaneously in Canada.

No part of this publication may be reproduced, stored in a retrieval system, or transmitted in any form or by any means, electronic, mechanical, photocopying, recording, scanning, or otherwise, except as permitted under Section 107 or 108 of the 1976 United States Copyright Act, without either the prior written permission of the Publisher, or authorization through payment of the appropriate per-copy fee to the Copyright Clearance Center, Inc., 222 Rosewood Drive, Danvers, MA 01923, (978) 750-8400, fax (978) 646-8600, or on the web at www.copyright.com. Requests to the Publisher for permission should be addressed to the Permissions Department, John Wiley & Sons, Inc., 111 River Street, Hoboken, NJ 07030, (201) 748-6011, fax (201) 748-6008, or online at http://www.wiley.com/go/permissions.

Limit of Liability/Disclaimer of Warranty: While the publisher and author have used their best efforts in preparing this book, they make no representations or warranties with respect to the accuracy or completeness of the contents of this book and specifically disclaim any implied warranties of merchantability or fitness for a particular purpose. No warranty may be created or extended by sales representatives or written sales materials. The advice and strategies contained herein may not be suitable for your situation. You should consult with a professional where appropriate. Neither the publisher nor author shall be liable for any loss of profit or any other commercial damages, including but not limited to special, incidental, consequential, or other damages.

Designations used by companies to distinguish their products are often claimed as trademarks. In all instances where John Wiley & Sons, Inc., is aware of a claim, the product names appear with an initial capital, or all capital letters. Readers, however, should contact the appropriate companies for more complete information regarding trademarks and registration.

For general information on our other products and services or for technical support, please contact our Customer Care Department within the United States at (800) 762-2974, outside the United States at (317) 572-3993 or fax (317) 572-4002.

Wiley also publishes its books in a variety of electronic formats. Some content that appears in print may not be available in electronic books. For more information about Wiley products, visit our web site at www.wiley.com.

Cloth edition: ISBN-10 0-471-70218-8; ISBN-13 978-0-471-70218-4

Cloth edition with CD-ROM: ISBN-10 0-471-70219-6; ISBN-13 978-0-471-70219-1

University edition: ISBN-10 0-471-70221-8; ISBN-13 978-0-471-70221-4

Workbook: ISBN-10 0-471-70216-1; ISBN-13 978-0-471-70216-0

CD-ROM: ISBN-10 0-471-70217-X; ISBN-13 978-0-471-70217-7

Web spreadsheet: ISBN-10 0-471-73389-X; ISBN-13 978-0-471-73389-8

Instructor's Manual: ISBN-10 0-471-70220-X; ISBN-13 978-0-471-70220-7

Printed in the United States of America.

10 9 8 7 6 5 4 3 2 1

About the Authors

Tim Koller is a partner in McKinsey's New York office. Tim has served clients in North America and Europe on corporate strategy and issues concerning capital markets, M&A transactions, and value-based management. He leads the firm's research activities in valuation and capital markets issues. He received his MBA from the University of Chicago.

Marc Goedhart is an associate principal in McKinsey's Amsterdam office. Marc has served clients across Europe on portfolio restructuring, issues concerning capital markets, and M&A transactions. He received a PhD in finance from Erasmus University Rotterdam.

David Wessels is an adjunct Professor of Finance and director of executive education at the Wharton School of the University of Pennsylvania. Named by *BusinessWeek* as one of America's top business school instructors, he teaches corporate valuation at the MBA and Executive MBA levels. David received his PhD from the University of California at Los Angeles.

Jeffrey P. Lessard is an associate professor of finance and accounting at the Rochester Institute of Technology. He received his PhD in finance from the Sam M. Walton College of Business at the University of Arkansas. Dr. Lessard's primary scholarly interests are in the areas of corporate valuation, the influence of the board of directors on the creation of shareholder value, portfolio performance, and performance and presentation standards in the investments industry.

Contents

Introduction

The purpose of any workbook is to actively engage the reader/learner in the transfer of knowledge from author to reader. Although there are many levels at which knowledge can be transferred, the *Valuation Workbook* endeavors to provide the following services:

1. A walk-through accompaniment to *Valuation: Measuring and Managing the Value of Companies, Fourth Edition.*
2. Rearrangement of ideas raised or concluded in the text to initiate and fuel discussion.
3. Tests of comprehension and skills.

Multiple-choice questions to pique your memory as you read the text. Lists and table completions force you to actively rearrange concepts explicitly or implicitly within the text. Calculation questions allow you to apply the skills deployed by the authors in accomplishing the analysis called valuation.

Our aim is to encourage you to question what you read against the background of your own business experience and think about new ways to analyze and approach valuation issues.

Part One

Questions

1

Why Maximize Value?

This chapter explains why maximizing shareholder value is the foundation of corporate management and the primary metric for corporate performance. Value comes in different forms and is perceived in various ways by an array of potential stakeholders. Important ideological and legal differences continue to exist among capitalist countries in the wake of the demise of communist economic systems. Investors, analysts, and management strive to understand the reasons behind the 40 percent decline in market value of equity assets between 1999 and 2002. The rise of hostile takeovers funded by high-yield debt along with anti-inflation monetary and fiscal policies spurred intense focus on earning high returns. Return expectations, understanding what drives corporate success, and volatility in the prices of common stock are at the core of management's corporate and ethical responsibilities. More and more employees hold equity in economies that quickly adapt to change. One common thread, the thread of maximizing shareholder value via maximizing stock price, ties each of these concepts together.

1. Shareholders a-nd wealth accumulation are most important in the _____, while _____ are more important determinants of value for continental Europe.

   A. Former communist countries, wealth and revenue growth.

   B. United States and United Kingdom; business continuity and inclusive stakeholder governance.

   C. Asia and Latin America; tax and social policy.

   D. Capital goods sector; representative directors and legal governance structures.

   E. Public Sector; tax and social policy.

2. Factors critical to the success of the shareholder model of value include which of the following:

    A. Convergence of incomes across classes of workers.

    B. Markets for corporate control.

    C. Insolvent social security systems.

    D. Emergence of the global economy.

    E. Increased household assets held as equity.

    F. Equity based management incentives.

    G. Political and social upheaval.

    H. Insolvency of social pension systems.

3. High-yield debt or junk bonds, as a major tool for restructuring companies, occasioned the rise of markets for corporate control during the 1980s.

    A. True, because more money could be found to fund takeovers.

    B. False, because more debt means less control over assets for shareholders.

    C. True, because debt structures required managers to quickly transform free cash flow into high market returns.

    D. False, because LBO transactions eventually fizzled after the U.S. Congress passed the Financial Institutions Reform, Recovery, and Enforcement Act of 1989.

4. Shareholders can align managers with enterprise goals by:

    A. Requiring more frequent and detailed reporting of operations.

    B. Replacing debt with equity, thus, forcing managers to invest in high-yield operational assets.

    C. Issuing stock options and share grants to managers for achieving various levels of performance.

    D. Reviewing management's hiring choices.

5. Ideological distinctions between labor and capital are blurring. Reasons and implications include:

    A. Real spending by households is falling.

    B. Increasing portions of pension fund assets are moving into equity.

    C. Monopolies are privatizing.

    D. Unionism is declining.

6. The arguments for public pensions to invest in market instruments include:

    A. Inducement of higher contribution premiums.

    B. Attractive returns can be found as funds transit from pay-as-you-go systems.

    C. Government policies are decreasing the retirement age.

    D. Savings need to derive from contribution premiums and investment returns.

7. Why should shareholder wealth be the most important metric of corporate performance?

    A. Equity holders have the most decision-making authority in the firm.

    B. Most employees have funded pensions.

    C. It shouldn't be. Job growth is the most important social goal on its own.

    D. Managers will limit investment in outdated strategies.

8. Identify three elements responsible for nearly all of the change in the broad market index caused by the bull market of 1980–2000.

    A. _____

    B. _____

    C. _____

9. Identify two recent examples where the capital markets misjudged corporate value.

    A. _____

    B. _____

10. Describe one of the fundamental performance factors that explains why U.S. companies are valued more highly than European or Asian companies.

    _____

    _____

2

The Value Manager

Chapter 1 argues for shareholder value as the primary performance metric. This chapter develops what this means in a practical way as Ralph Demsky walks into a company that needs managerial attention. First, he focuses on the portfolio of opportunities and disasters that comprise EG Corporation. Then, he embarks on a systematic quest to discern where and how value is either created or destroyed in each of EG's business units. Finally, he takes steps to restructure both the corporate performance and culture.

1. The most important trait of a value manager is:
   A. To be a coach.
   B. To focus on long-run cash flow returns and incremental value.
   C. To adopt a dispassionate view of corporate activities.
   D. To institutionalize value management throughout the organization.
   E. To provide each stakeholder group an opportunity to influence both the corporate culture and future corporate strategies.

2. Identify and define the three steps necessary to develop a value management philosophy.
   A. _____
   B. _____
   C. _____

3. The situation that best describes EG Corporation as Ralph Demsky becomes CEO is:

   A. A poorly performing, but otherwise well-managed and rationalized set of related businesses.

   B. An average corporation comprised of consumer goods, manufacturing, service, property, and finance companies.

   C. A corporation with some spectacular performers, especially in the finance and manufacturing businesses.

   D. A corporation that was fairly well managed requiring minor adjustments to demonstrate its full potential.

   E. A poorly managed corporation demonstrating no coherent strategy for position, growth, or resource allocation.

4. In addition to the corporate strategy hexagon DCF valuations, identify three other analyses Ralph's team conducted in the evaluation on EG Corporation:

   A. _____

   B. _____

   C. _____

5. Identify the main virtues and failings of Consumerco, Woodco, and Foodco:

	Strength	Weakness
Consumerco		
Woodco		
Foodco		

6. What are the external analyst's concerns with respect to EG's performance?

   A. _____

   B. _____

   C. _____

7. How did Ralph posture the restructuring project?

   A. Kept it quiet so that no one would be upset over half-baked conclusions and rumors.

   B. Included only financial analysts to speed up the work.

   C. Broadcast the project across the entire company to allay suspicion and include everyone's ideas.

   D. Selected key business leaders along with analysts to take an open-minded but hard-nosed look at sources of value.

   E. Assign the primary situational review and corporate reengineering to external consultants with an expertise in corporate turnarounds.

8. List the components (hexagon), expected products (performance analyses, scenarios, etc.) and significant results (for each division) of Ralph's approach to analyzing EG's value:

Components	Products	Results
Current valuation		
As is value		
Value with internal improvements		
Value with external improvements		
New growth opportunities		
Value from financial engineering		

9. Which statement follows from Ralph's restructuring plan of action?

   A. Maintain investment-grade debt rating, capitalize on Consumerco success, and sell Foodco.

   B. Abandon Woodco consolidation, maintain headquarters' control, and expand Foodco.

C. Sell property and newspaper businesses, push headquarters functions into divisions, and recapitalize by borrowing at lower debt rating.

D. Develop investor communication strategy, double Consumerco value and maintain headquarters staff to oversee the restructuring plan.

10. Outline Ralph's steps to manage EG's value:

A. _____

B. _____

C. _____

D. _____

E. _____

11. How will Ralph put value planning into action?

A. Require everyone to focus on growth in sales and earnings.

B. Focus on what drives value for their business-growth, margin, or capital.

C. Focus on investment in R&D.

D. Reduce reliance on staff functions.

12. What measures best support Ralph's approach to value planning?

A. Return on investment (ROI) since this is what shareholders crave.

B. Payback since this measures how fast a strategy returns cash flow.

C. Capital growth since this is the measure of the size of the wealth opportunity.

D. Economic profit since this measures how operations exceed shareholder expectations for return.

E. Changes in EPS since this is what the stock market values.

3

Fundamental Principles of Value Creation

Previous chapters argued that shareholder value and systematic deployment within complex organizations require a revolution in thinking: All planning should revolve around a notion of economic profit. This chapter expands on this notion with an extension of period-to-period economic profit into discounted cash flow and the importance of managing value drivers over time.

1. How does economic profit grow?
   A. Increase invested capital.
   B. Increase shareholder returns expectations (cost of capital).
   C. Decrease shareholder returns expectations (cost of capital).
   D. Increase return on invested capital.

2. How can shutting down a low-profit division actually lower economic profit?
   A. It doesn't, because average return on invested capital (ROIC) will rise.
   B. It can, because the amount of invested capital drops.
   C. It doesn't, because investor return expectations are not changed.
   D. It does, if the low-profit division still outperforms investor return expectations.

3. Why is period-to-period economic profit insufficient to measure performance?

   A. It isn't insufficient since all elements of value creation are represented.

   B. It is insufficient because future performance is not impounded into the metric.

   C. It is insufficient because the cost of capital is not included in the calculation.

   D. It isn't insufficient because the cost of capital is included in the calculation.

4. How are decisions in real and financial markets different?

   A. They really aren't different because each depends on the maximization of future value.

   B. They really aren't different because real market performance is mimicked and replicated in efficient financial markets.

   C. They are different because real market, discounted cash flow maximization must be augmented by financial market preferences for exceeding expectations of intrinsic value.

   D. They are different because real market value optimization does not take into account financial market systematic risk.

5. Why is it important not to over- or underestimate stock market expectations of intrinsic value?

   A. If you overestimate, you may be subject to a takeover.

   B. If you overestimate, you may lack credibility.

   C. If you underestimate, you may be subject to a takeover.

   D. If you underestimate, you may lack credibility.

6. Other than measuring performance and being attuned to market perception of value, what else is needed to succeed in growing a profitable business?

   A. _____

   B. _____

7. Identify the five key lessons of value creation.

   A. _____

   B. _____

   C. _____

D. _____

E. _____

8. Why should Fred be more concerned with economic profit than returns on capital?

9. Firms A and B are constant growth firms, identical in every aspect except that the ROIC for A is 15 percent and B is 5 percent. Assume that management is in the process of establishing an investment rate of either 40 percent or 60 percent for each firm. Compute the estimated value for each investment rate for each firm given the following information. What conclusions should be drawn with respect to the relationship of WACC to ROIC?

	A	B
NOPLAT at $t = 1$	$5,000	$5,000
WACC	10%	10%
Investment rate	1. 40%	1. 40%
	2. 60%	2. 60%
Return on new capital	15%	5%

4

Do Fundamentals Really Drive the Stock Market?

The second half of the 1990s witnessed the S&P 500 Index more than tripling in value to an all-time high of almost 1,500. Previous unknowns became stock market superstars, along with the "New Economy" and dot-com entrants. The market then crashed. In the aftermath of these market gyrations, people began to question whether long-held finance theories could really explain such dramatic swings in share prices. Some asserted that the stock markets lead lives of their own detached from the basics of economic growth and business profitability. New valuation models were put forward to explain how the market had changed and how the market could no longer be considered rational and efficient. Should we abandon the discounted cash flow (DCF) valuations described in Chapter 3 and view the stock market as an arena where emotions rule?

1. Define market efficiency.

   _____

   _____

2. Are financial markets efficient? Provide support for your contention.

   _____

   _____

3. Identify the basic economic laws that direct market behavior. What evidence exists that support the existence of these laws?

   _____

   _____

4. Identify three conditions put forth by behavioral finance theorists that explain why markets may fail to reflect economic fundamentals.

   A. _____

   B. _____

   C. _____

5. Identify four examples of how a corporate manager might benefit from intrinsic value deviations by better timing the implementation of strategic decisions.

   A. _____

   B. _____

   C. _____

   D. _____

5

Frameworks for Valuation

Having been (we hope) convinced of the worthiness of shareholder valuation and discounted cash flow in particular, this chapter proposes a set of formulas consistent with valuation principles. A company's value is driven, first, by its ability to earn a return on invested capital (ROIC) greater than its weighted average cost of capital (WACC), and second, by its ability to grow. High returns and growth result in high cash flows, which in turn drives value. Chapter 5 focuses on two valuation approaches: enterprise DCF and discounted economic profit. When applied correctly, both valuation methods yield the same results; however, each model has certain benefits in practice. Enterprise DCF remains the favorite of many practitioners and academics because it relies solely on the flow of cash in and out of the company, rather than on accounting-based earnings. Discounted economic profit is gaining in popularity because of its close link to economic theory and competitive strategy.

1. List the components of the enterprise discounted cash flow model.

    A. _____

    B. _____

    C. _____

2. Define free cash flow, net investment, and investment rate:

    A. Free cash flow: _____

    B. Net investment: _____

    C. Investment rate: _____

3. Identify four process steps necessary to value equity using the enterprise model:

   A. _____

   B. _____

   C. _____

   D. _____

4. Identify the components of the economic profit model and reconcile them with the discounted cash flow model.

   A. _____

   B. _____

   C. _____

   D. _____

5. What must a company do to increase its value? Outline three action plans that relate to ROIC, WACC, growth, capital, and NOPLAT.

   A. _____

   B. _____

   C. _____

6. Compare and contrast the free cash flow and economic profit models of value. Use three firms as an illustration: one firm earns 10 percent and reinvests 100 percent of NOPLAT into incremental capital (beyond replacement capital expenditures), another earns 12.5 percent and reinvests 80 percent of NOPLAT into capital, a third earns 12.5 percent and reinvests 200 percent of NOPLAT into capital; each firm has a cost of capital of 10%. Use the following template for the analysis:

	X	Y	Z
ROIC			
WACC			
Growth			
IR			
NOPLAT			
Net Investment			
FCF			
NOPLAT increase			
ROIC new capital			
EP new capital			

7. Outline the steps in a valuation study.

A. _____

B. _____

C. _____

D. _____

E. _____

6

Thinking about Return on Invested Capital and Growth

A fully developed discounted cash flow model can be complex. Models that forecast each line item on the income statement and balance sheet can include hundreds of numbers, if not thousands. It is all too easy to forget the fundamentals: A company's value depends on its return on invested capital (ROIC) and its ability to grow. All other considerations—gross margins, cash tax rates, collection periods, inventory turns—are, well, just details.

1. Identify and discuss three sources of competitive advantage that could lead to increases in ROIC.

   A. _____

   B. _____

   C. _____

7

Analyzing Historical
Performance

Understanding a company's past is essential for forecasting its future. For that reason, we begin the valuation process by analyzing historical performance. Since the financial statements are not designed for valuation, historical analysis can be challenging. To properly evaluate a company's performance, it is therefore necessary to rearrange the accounting statements, dig for new information in the footnotes, and, where information is missing, make informed assumptions. Only then will the company's previous performance, competitive position, and ability to generate cash in the future come into focus.

1. What are the starting points and ultimate goals of a comprehensive system for the analysis of historical performance?

   A. Starting points: _____

   B. Ultimate goals: _____

2. Identify and explain the key steps that occur to restate the company's balance sheet and income statement.

   A. _____

   B. _____

   C. _____

   D. _____

3. What are the determinants of ROIC?

A. _____

B. _____

C. _____

The following data is for BMI, Inc.:

	2004	2005
Current assets	$ 863	$ 896
Current liabilities	710	818
Debt in current liabilities	1	39
Long-term debt	506	408
Total assets	2,293	2,307
Capital expenditures	111	117
Change in deferred taxes	(29)	(20)
Sales	4,056	4,192
Operating expenses	3,307	3,408
General expenses	562	528
Depreciation	139	136
Investment income	5	6
Interest expense	39	30
Miscellaneous income, net	(25)	(4)
Income taxes	(7)	41
Marginal tax rate	64%	45%

The following six questions refer to BMI, Inc.

4. Compute invested capital and NOPLAT.

	2004	2005
Invested Capital Statement		
Working capital		
Long term assets	——	——
Operating invested capital	══	══
Debt		
Equity		
NOPLAT Statement		
Sales		
Operating expenses		
General expenses		
Depreciation	——	——
EBIT		
Taxes on EBIT		
Change in deferred taxes	——	——
NOPLAT	══	══
Provision for income taxes		
Tax shield on interest expense		
Tax on investment income		
Tax on non-operating income	——	——
Taxes on EBIT	══	══

5. Reconcile the NOPLAT statement to Net Income using the following template:

	2004	2005
Net Income Statement		
Sales		
Operating expenses		
General expenses		
Depreciation	———	———
EBIT		
Investment income		
Interest expense		
Miscellaneous, net	———	———
Earnings before taxes		
Income taxes	———	———
Net income (before extra items)	═══	═══
Reconciliation to Net Income Statement		
Net income		
Add: Increase in deferred taxes	———	———
Adjusted net income		
Add: Interest expense after tax	———	———
Income available to investors		
Less: Investment income after tax		
Less: Non-operating income after tax	———	———
NOPLAT	═══	═══

6. Produce a ROIC tree with the following template:

	2004	2005
ROIC Tree		
ROIC = (1 − EBIT cash tax rate)		
× Pretax ROIC		
= EBIT/sales		
× Sales/invested capital		
EBIT/sales = 1 − (Operating expenses/sales		
+ General expenses/sales		
+ Depreciation/sales)		
Sales/invested capital		
= 1/(Operating working capital/sales		
+ Long term operating assets/sales)		

7. Present a free cash flow statement with the following template:

	2005
Free Cash Flow Statement	
NOPLAT	
Depreciation	————
Gross cash flow	════
Increase in operating working capital	
Capital expenditures	————
Gross investment	════
Free cash flow	════
Non-operating cash flow	————
Cash flow available to investors	════

8. Prepare an economic profit statement. Assume an 11.1 percent weighted average cost of capital.

	2005
Economic Profit	
NOPLAT	
Capital charge	____
Economic Profit	====

9. Compare and contrast the free cash flow and economic profit statements.

8

Forecasting Performance

You've analyzed the historical record, researched patterns of change in the firm and its markets, estimated the riskiness of the firm as indicated by the return to compensate investors, now we look to the future. The future depends critically on the strategic perspective of the firm as well as the various horizons the firm sets for itself. There is at least a near and far term.

1. Outline the six steps in producing a firm's financial forecast.

A. _____

B. _____

C. _____

D. _____

E. _____

F. _____

2. It has been said repeatedly that adding value translates into an ROIC greater than a WACC. How do each of the following lead to competitive advantages in an evaluation of strategic position?

Buyers

Suppliers

Technology

Government

New entrants

Substitute products/services

3. Discuss how customer segmentation, business system, and industry structure analysis contribute to a better understanding of the value-added for the firm.

Customer segmentation

Business system

Industry structure analysis

4. Discuss how capital structure affects corporate valuation. Use the enterprise DCF model to illustrate your position.

5. Given the historical data, forecast International Machine Tools, Inc.'s (IMT) FCF for the following two scenarios:

A. *Aggressive (AG):* IMT introduces significant changes and increases to its product line and ability to meet technological change in the industry. Goal: Improve all expense structures at high levels of sales growth over the near term; operating expense/sales of 74 percent, 73 percent, 73 percent for three years, SG&A/sales of 16 percent, depreciation/sales of 2.5 percent, taxes of 40 percent, working capital/sales of 18.75 percent, net fixed assets of 24 percent, and 3 years of sales growth of 40 percent per year.

B. *Conservative (CO):* IMT is barely able to hold its own in the global arena of faster-paced technological change and customer demands. Goal: Maintain historical sales, operating and general expense structures; operating expense/sales of 74 percent in perpetuity, SG&A/sales of 18.6 percent, taxes of 40 percent, working capital/sales of 18.15 percent, net fixed assets of 24 percent, and 3 years of sales growth at 20 percent per year.

International Machine Tools Inc. (IMT)

	2000	2001	2002	2003	2004
Current assets	499	489	443	429	484
Current liabilities	240	236	255	237	369
Debt in current liabilities	25	12	7	21	78
Long-term debt	218	200	244	207	236
Total assets	686	693	598	579	730
Capital expenditures	34	34	16	18	23
Change in deferred taxes	4	(5)	3	2	2
Sales	851	838	754	789	1,029
Operating expenses	626	624	579	592	765
General expenses	151	157	132	134	191
Depreciation	23	24	24	21	26
Investment income	4	2	2	3	2
Interest expense	22	20	19	19	16
Miscellaneous income, net	3	(33)	(75)	–	(70)
Income taxes	18	4	10	11	8

6. Use the following template to construct and discuss forecasts for the given historical data; forecast IMT's FCF for the following two scenarios:

Driver	Low Growth: Conservative	High Growth: Aggressive
Operative expenses/sales		
SGA/Sales		
Growth		
Other		

9

Estimating
Continuing Value

1. What are three common errors executives make when estimating continuing value using the value driver formulas?

    A. _____

    B. _____

    C. _____

2. Identify and define four technical considerations to be analyzed when estimating continuing value using the value driver formula.

    A. _____

    B. _____

    C. _____

    D. _____

3. A client explains that her firm's value must be affected by the choice of explicit forecast horizon. Build a model to test her claim. NOPLAT, depreciation, and gross investment for year 1 have been forecasted to be $10.00, $2.50, and $13.61, respectively.

    A. To evaluate your client's claim, first assume a short horizon of three years.

    B. Compare the results of this three-year horizon to a five-year forecasted horizon. The company's management team forecasted ROIC for years 1 to 3 to be 18 percent and 11 percent thereafter. The company executives also forecasted NOPLAT to grow at 20 percent for years 1 to 3 and to decline to a continuing growth rate of 7 percent thereafter. Finally, the management team has estimated an initial WACC of 14 percent for years 1 to 3, and declining to 12 percent after the initial forecasted period.

C. Compare your computed value for both time horizons. Provide an explanation of your results.

Given:

Assumptions	Years 1–3 (%)		Years 4+ (%)
ROIC	18		11
Growth	20		7
WACC	14		12

3-Year Horizon	1	2	3	CV Base
NOPLAT				
Depreciation				
Gross cash flow				
Gross investment				
Free cash flow				
Discount factor				
Present value FCF				
PV FCF 1–3				
PV CV				
Total Value				

5-Year Horizon	1	2	3	4	5	CV Base
NOPLAT						
Depreciation						
Gross cash flow						
Gross investment						
Free cash flow						
Discount factor						
Present value FCF						
PV FCF 1–3						
PV CV						
Total Value						

4. Your client remains skeptical. Why use two different representations of value—free cash flow and economic profit? Show her that the present value of economic profit plus beginning invested capital equals the present value of free cash flows.

5. Demonstrate for your client the equivalence between free cash flow and economic profit representations of value with a model similar to the three-year horizon model. Discuss the similarities, differences, and usefulness of each representation. Use the following template and assumptions:

Assumptions	Year 1–3 (%)	Year 4+ (%)
ROIC	18.00	15.75
Growth	20.00	5.00
WACC	14.00	12.00

3-Year Horizon	1	2	3	CV Base
NOPLAT				
Net investment				
Free cash flow				
Beginning IC				
Net investment				
New IC				
NOPLAT				
Capital charge				
Economic profit				
Discount factor				
Present value FCF				
Present value EP				
PV FCF 1–3				
PV CV FCF				
Total Value				
PV EP 1–3				
PV CV				
IC				
Total Value				

6. Complete the valuation of International Machine Tools, Inc. using data from previous chapters. Include a range of possible outcomes based on growth versus the ROIC positioning of the firm. Assume 33.7 million

outstanding shares and an initial beta of 1.73. A template follows with example assumptions:

	2001	2002	2003	2004	2005
Financial data input					
Current assets	$ 2,595	$ 2,615	$ 2,916	$ 2,645	$ 4,559
Current liabilities	1,764	2,490	3,020	2,648	4,191
Debt in current liabilities	0	0	0	0	0
Long-term debt	7,052	6,817	6,460	6,928	8,831
Total assets	12,335	12,818	12,950	12,700	16,897
Capital expenditures	1,503	1,564	892	951	2,609
Change in deferred taxes	10	14	100	38	73
Sales	14,313	13,024	13,094	13,342	17,977
Operating expenses	9,794	9,798	10,209	10,231	13,333
General expenses	1,406	1,475	1,296	1,204	1,670
Depreciation	984	996	1,017	997	1,013
Investment income	—	—	128	24	355
Interest expense	432	459	465	443	495
Miscellaneous income, net	—	(5)	(60)	(15)	—
Income taxes	679	135	106	202	705
Beta	1.33	1.33	1.33	1.33	1.33

	2001	2002	2003	2004	2005
Invested capital statement					
Working capital					
Long-term assets					
Operating invested capital					
Net investment					
Debt					
Equity					
NOPLAT statement					
Sales					
Operating expenses					
General expenses					
Depreciation					
EBIT					
Taxes on EBIT					
Change in deferred taxes					
NOPLAT					
Provision for income taxes					
Tax shield on interest expense					
Tax on investment income					
Tax on non-operating income					
Taxes on EBIT					
Net income statement					
Sales					
Operating expenses					
General expenses					
Depreciation					
EBIT					
Investment income					
Investment expense					
Miscellaneous, net					
Earnings before taxes					
Income taxes					
Net income (before extra items)					
Tax rate					

(continued)

	2001	2002	2003	2004	2005
Reconciliation to net income statement					
Net income					
Add: increase in deferred taxes					
Adjusted net income					
Add: Interest expense after tax					
Income available to investors					
Less: Interest income after tax					
Less: Non-operating income after tax					
NOPLAT					
ROIC tree					
ROIC					
= (1 − EBIT cash tax rate) × Pretax ROIC					
= EBIT/Sales × Sales/Invested capital					
EBIT/Sales = 1 − (Operating expenses/Sales + General expenses/Sales + Depreciation/Sales)					
Sales/Invested capital = 1 /(Operating working capital/Sales + Long-term operating assets/Sales)					
Change in deferred tax/Sales					
Free cash flow statement					
NOPLAT					
Depreciation					
Gross cash flow					

(continued)

	2001	2002	2003	2004	2005
Increase in operating working capital					
Capital expenditures		___	___	___	___
Gross investment		═══	═══	═══	═══
Free cash flow		═══	═══	═══	═══
Non-operating cash flow		___	___	___	___
Cash flow available to investors		═══	═══	═══	═══
Cost of capital					
Beta					
Debt/invested capital					
Equity/invested capital					
Cost of debt					
Cost of equity					
Weighted average cost of capital					
Economic profit					
NOPLAT					
Capital charge		___	___	___	___
Economic profit		═══	═══	═══	═══

10

Estimating the Cost
of Capital

To value a company using enterprise DCF, we discount free cash flow by the weighted average cost of capital (WACC). The weighted average cost of capital represents the opportunity cost that investors face for investing their funds in one particular business instead of others with similar risk. The most important principle underlying successful implementation of the cost of capital is consistency between the components of WACC and free cash flow. Since free cash flow is the cash flow available to all financial investors (debt, equity, and hybrid securities), the company's WACC must include the required return for each investor.

1. Identify and describe five key principles of computing WACC.

   A. _____

   B. _____

   C. _____

   D. _____

   E. _____

2. Identify three key characteristics of the raw data needed for computing the CAPM.

   A. _____

   B. _____

   C. _____

3. Present, in its simplest form, the WACC formula.

4. Identify the steps necessary to estimate the cost of capital.

   A. _____

   B. _____

   C. _____

   D. _____

5. What approaches can be used to develop market value weights?

   A. _____

   B. _____

   C. _____

6. Suppose you can issue one of two bonds each carrying a coupon of 10 percent of face value payable at the end of each of two years. The principle repayment for one bond is 100 percent at the end of year two; for the other bond, it is 50 percent at the end of year one and 50 percent at the end of year two. The sinking fund earns escrow interest of 10 percent. What is the pretax cost of capital (yield or internal rate of return) on the two bonds if face value is $1,000? Use the following template:

Bond 1	0	1	2
Interest			
Principal			
Net cash flow			
Yield to maturity			

Bond 2	0	1	2
Interest			
Principal			
Net cash flow			
Yield to maturity			

7. What is the effect of taxes on the analysis of the cost of capital of the two bonds described above? Assume a 40 percent tax on ordinary income (revenue and cost components). Use the following template:

Bond 1	0	1	2
Interest received			
Interest paid			
Taxes			
Principal			
Net cash flow			
Yield to maturity			

Bond 2	0	1	2
Interest received			
Interest paid			
Taxes			
Principal			
Net cash flow			
Yield to maturity			

8. Newcome Steel's balance sheet shows a total of $30 million in long-term debt with a coupon rate of 9 percent. The yield to maturity on this debt is 7.3 percent, and the debt has a total current market value of $35 million. The company has 10 million shares of stock outstanding. The value of common stock and retained earnings presented in the balance sheet is $45 million. The current stock price is quoted $7.50 per share. The current return required by stockholders is estimated at 11.3 percent. The tax rate is 40 percent. Given the company has a target capital structure of 40 percent debt and 60 percent equity, estimate the WACC for Newcome.

9. LPJ has no growth opportunities, thus LPJ pays out all of its earnings as dividends. LPJ has a capital structure, based on market values, that consists of 20 percent debt and 80 percent equity. The yield to maturity on existing debt instruments averages 7.3 percent. If LPJ were to adjust its debt structure, staff analysts estimate that the YTM on existing debt instruments would increase by .75 percent. The risk-free rate is 6 percent and the market is expected to yield 11.3 percent. Currently, the company's cost of equity, which is based on the CAPM, is 12.36 percent and its tax rate is 40 percent.

   What is LPJ's cost of capital given a change in its capital structure to 50 percent debt and 50 percent equity?

   A. _____

   B. _____

   C. _____

   D. _____

   E. _____

   F. _____

11

Calculating and Interpreting Results

1. Identify the three steps needed to compute the present value of operations.

   A. _____

   B. _____

   C. _____

2. Detail the final steps needed to produce a company's value.

   A. _____

   B. _____

3. Identify four categories of nonequity claims.

   A. _____

   B. _____

   C. _____

   D. _____

4. If a parent company is not able to consolidate a subsidiary's financial position, explain how the degree of equity ownership impacts the parent company's cash flow position.

Ownership Position <20%	Ownership Position 20% to 50%

5. Identify the steps that should be taken to verify the results obtained from estimating enterprise value.

    A. _____

    B. _____

    C. _____

6. From a manager's perspective, what is the purpose of computing the firm's enterprise value?

_____

_____

_____

12

Using Multiples
for Valuation

Discounted cash flow analysis is the most accurate and flexible method for valuing projects, divisions, and companies. Any analysis, however, is only as accurate as the forecasts it relies on. Errors in estimating the key ingredients of corporate value—such as a company's ROIC, growth rate, and WACC—can lead to mistakes in valuation and, ultimately, to strategic errors. The proper use of a multiples valuation should support the valuation conclusions drawn from enterprise- or economic-based valuation models.

1. Why is it important that management perform a supplemental analysis employing a relative valuation model?

   _____

   _____

   _____

2. Identify the four best practices for using multiples practices applied to the construction of a valuation multiple.

   A. _____

   B. _____

   C. _____

   D. _____

3. Compare and contrast the relative P/E valuation model to the DCF valuation model.

The Relative P/E Valuation Model   **The DCF Valuation Model**

13

Performance Measurement

Performance measurement looks at value creation from a managerial perspective: managing performance to increase ROIC and growth; creating value through mergers, acquisitions, and divestitures; using capital structure to support value creation; and communicating effectively with investors to ensure that the company's stock price reflects its intrinsic value.

1. Identify the three questions around which performance measurement should be organized.

   A. _____

   B. _____

   C. _____

2. What is meant by the implied P/E on debt model? Assume a company borrows at 7.2 percent and gets a tax benefit of 35 percent for its borrowing. Explain how changing a company's leverage could be used to meet P/E or earnings targets.

   _____

   _____

   _____

3. Identify the difference between short-term and medium-term performance metrics.

_____

_____

_____

4. Identify the three categories of short-term performance metrics.

    A. _____

    B. _____

    C. _____

5. Identify the three categories of medium-term performance metrics.

    A. _____

    B. _____

    C. _____

6. What is the relationship between ROIC and economic profit? Develop a rationale that will lead a manager to conclude that economic profit is superior to ROIC.

_____

_____

_____

14

Performance Management

Companies establish systems to ensure that decisions are consistent with short-term and long-term objectives and that the management team can clearly see how those myriad decisions affect value creation. Performance management systems, typically include long-term strategic plans, short-term budgets, capital budgeting systems, performance reporting and reviews, and compensation systems. Successful value creation requires that all components of these management systems are aligned to the company's strategy so as to encourage decisions that maximize value.

1. Identify and define the five components of an effective performance management system.

   A. _____

   B. _____

   C. _____

   D. _____

   E. _____

2. How does an effective performance management system differ from early value-based management systems?

   _____

   _____

   _____

3. What is the difference among a value driver, value metric, and milestone? Describe the relationship among value drivers, value metrics, and milestones.

_____

_____

_____

4. What are the advantages/disadvantages of tailored value drivers versus the balanced scorecard?

_____

_____

_____

5. Why is it important for a manager to understand a business's value drivers and how each driver affects value?

_____

_____

_____

6. Identify the two-step process employed to determine a company's value drivers.

   A. _____

   B. _____

7. What is the purpose of creating a value tree analysis? Identify the four key filters to identify the value drivers for creating a company's value tree diagram.

   A. _____

   B. _____

   C. _____

   D. _____

8. What is the purpose of identifying an appropriate benchmark? Describe five types of benchmarks.

A. _____

B. _____

C. _____

D. _____

E. _____

15

Creating Value through Mergers and Acquisitions

Mergers and acquisitions are among the many strategies firms use. Most executives will be involved at least in the analysis of potential candidates or the consideration of various overtures. A merger or acquisition becomes a comprehensive application of how to make value happen.

1. What are the reasons companies that employ M&A win or lose.

Winners	Losers

2. Outline the steps for a successful merger or acquisition.

   A. _____

   B. _____

C. _____

D. _____

E. _____

3. How can a company establish a clear vision for value creation that will work best in a merger or acquisition?

A. _____

B. _____

C. _____

4. How can M&A affect a company's relations with its customer?

A. _____

B. _____

C. _____

5. Detail a candidate screening method.

A. _____

B. _____

C. _____

6. Describe potential synergies across the business system useful in analyzing M&A candidates.

Business System Component	Potential Synergy

7. Define three steps to successfully manage postmerger issues:

Issue	Resolution

8. Compare and contrast mergers with joint ventures using the following characteristics:

Characteristic	Merger/Aquisition	Joint Venture
Overlap		
Ownership split		
Decision making		
Time frame		

16

Creating Value through Divestitures

Divestitures, like mergers and acquisitions, tend to occur in waves. Evidence shows that divestitures create value for corporations, both in the short term, around their announcement, and in the long term. Furthermore, companies employing a balanced portfolio approach of both acquisitions and divestitures have outperformed companies that rarely divested.

1. Identify five factors that complicate a manager's decision to divest a business unit.

   A. _____

   B. _____

   C. _____

   D. _____

   E. _____

2. Identify and describe two private transaction and two public transaction approaches to corporate divesture. When are private transactions likely to create more value than public transactions?

Transaction Approaches to Corporate Divesture	
Private	**Public**
1.	1.
2.	2.

3. Why might a corporation wish to divest its mature business units to acquire business units in either the start-up or expansion phase of an industry's life cycle?

_____

_____

_____

4. Describe the key reasons why divesting a business can create value for shareholders even when the business is still in the early stages of its life cycle.

_____

_____

_____

17

Capital Structure

1. Define optimal capital structure. What is the relationship between optimal capital structure, corporate value, and cost of capital?

_____

_____

_____

2. Academics argue that every corporation has an optimal capital structure. Most firms have a debt position consistent to an S&P financial risk rating between BBB and A. When you evaluate companies, you note that many companies carry essentially no long-term debt and only a minimal short-term debt position in their capital structure (review the balance sheet of United Microelectronics and Symantec). Provide an explanation as to why well-managed and profitable companies appear to undervalue the benefits associated with an optimal capital structure.

_____

_____

_____

3. What is the primary benefit of a company in issuing debt to finance its asset base? What is the primary cost associated with a company's debt position?

_____

_____

_____

4. Identify and quantify the relationship between an increase in the debt position of a company and its estimated cost of equity.

_____

_____

_____

5. Outline a process a manager should employ to establish an effective capital structure target.

_____

_____

_____

6. Describe the importance of the pecking order theory for managing the capital structure of a company as it relates to both short-term, tactical financing decisions and long-term, strategic decisions.

_____

_____

_____

18

Investor
Communications

Executives spend a large and growing portion of their time on investor communications, yet they are frustrated by the amount of time it takes and the nature of their interactions with investors. Executives are obsessed with their company's share price, and worry constantly that it isn't high enough, or that markets don't understand their company sufficiently. Until recently, companies have approached investor communications in an ad hoc way. Executives receive advice from investor relations consultants, whose background is typically in public relations rather than finance. The academic community has only recently started to research investor composition and communications.

1. Identify and describe two primary benefits a systematic approach to investor communications provides a manager.

    A. _____

    B. _____

2. Identify and describe the three key elements of a well-defined investment story.

    A. _____

    B. _____

    C. _____

3. Compare and contrast intrinsic value and market price. If the capital markets are efficient, what should be the relationship between intrinsic value and market price?

_____

_____

_____

_____

4. Define the term *transparency* as it relates to corporate investor communications.

_____

_____

_____

5. If transparency is a significant benefit, identify where too much transparency might lead to a reduction in corporate value. Consider in your answer how too much transparency could lead to a decline in a firm's competitive position and enterprise value.

_____

_____

_____

6. The general consensus among academics is that the capital markets are efficient. If the capital markets are efficient, identify the potential value gained by having management establish an effective investor communications department?

_____

_____

_____

19

Valuing Multibusiness Companies

Most large companies are in multiple businesses. Some companies are quite diverse, but, even companies with a narrower focus often compete in multiple segments. If each business unit's financial characteristics (growth and return on capital) are significantly different, it is best to analyze and value each unit separately and then sum the parts to estimate the value of the entire company.

1. Identify three unique issues associated with valuing a multibusiness company.

   A. _____

   B. _____

   C. _____

2. Outline a two-step process to identify the target capital structure of a business unit within a multibusiness company.

   _____

   _____

   _____

3. Chapter 19 suggests that business unit valuation might provide managerial benefits, such as a better prioritization both of a manager's time and efforts and of corporate resource allocation. Discuss how business unit

valuation might lead to better alignment of corporate priorities with value creation.

_____

_____

_____

4. If the capital markets are efficient, should a conglomerate discount exist? Assuming that the capital markets are efficient, provide an alternative explanation for the existence of a conglomerate discount.

_____

_____

_____

5. When estimating enterprise value, the firm's cost of capital is a critical driver of value. Explain how financial and operating risks impact both the company's capital structure and a business unit's target capital structure. What influence do operating and financial synergies have on the component cost estimates of these capital structures?

_____

_____

_____

20

Valuing Flexibility

1. Present the general decision rule for NPV.

_____

_____

_____

2. Identify four options a company may employ to adjust production.

   A. _____

   B. _____

   C. _____

   D. _____

3. Identify two primary methods for valuating flexibility.

   A. _____

   B. _____

4. Outline the four-step process for valuing flexibility.

   A. _____

   B. _____

   C. _____

   D. _____

5. Identify the two most important real options available to a manager evaluating investment decisions.

   A. _____

   B. _____

6. Consider the project described in Exhibit 20.4. One could argue that the flexibility to defer the investment decision until the trial results are known reduces risk because the adverse outcome of a $55 loss can be avoided. But we know that to correctly value the flexibility in a DTA approach, we need to use a discount rate of 15.5 percent, which is above the 10 percent cost of capital for the project without flexibility. How can lower risk lead to a higher discount rate? Explain.

   _____

   _____

   _____

21

Cross-Border Valuation

With the recent revision of IFRS becoming effective at the beginning of 2005, the major differences between IFRS and U.S. GAAP have disappeared. However, when analyzing longer-term historical performance, you may find that former differences still have an impact because companies usually provide only a few years of results based on similar accounting principles for comparison purposes.

1. To what extent are NOPLAT, invested capital and free cash flow for a company influenced by accounting standards?

2. List several hurdles to restatement of foreign accounting statements:

    A. _____

    B. _____

    C. _____

    D. _____

3. Perform the following operations given you can: borrow USD 1 today and earn USD 1.076 in one year. Borrow GBP/USD .66997 today and earn GBP/USD (.66997)(1.065) or .71352 in one year.

    A. In one year, GBP/USD is expected to be _____.

    B. Thus, USD equivalent earned in one year is GBP _____/GBP/USD _____ or _____.

    C. Your conclusion about risk-free rates across heavily arbitraged currency borders is _____.

4. To address international differences in taxation, identify four questions that need to be examined:

A. _____

B. _____

C. _____

D. _____

5. 90-day Euro investments provide a 9 percent annualized return (2.25 percent quarterly) whereas USD, 90-day investments of equivalent risk provide a 6 percent annualized return (1.5 percent quarterly). If the Euro equals 1.53 USD in the 90-day forward market, what is the spot exchange rate given interest rate parity holds?

6. A year ago, LPJ, Inc had inventory in Germany valued at 6,320,000 Euros. The exchange rate for dollars to Euros was 1 Euro = 1.15 USD. This year, the exchange rate is 1 Euro = 0.87 USD. The inventory in Europe is on the books at 6,320,000 Euros. Identify any gain or loss in inventory value in USD as a result of the change in exchange rates?

22

Valuation in
Emerging Markets

The valuation of nominal versus real cash flows headlines the many issues addressed in this chapter. Cash flows for emerging market companies are often affected by abrupt changes in open economies, monetary and fiscal policy, spot and forward movements in capital and foreign currency markets, as well as a host of problems associated with liquidity, sovereign debt, repatriation of dividends and local taxation, import-export quota, and exchange rate translation. The problems following focus on real and nominal cash flow forecasts and their valuation.

1. Identify three effects of volatile inflation on estimating cash flows:

    A. _____

    B. _____

    C. _____

2. Identify and describe three adjustments to the enterprise DCF and economic profit when attempting to establish the value of a company located in an emerging market.

    A. _____

    B. _____

    C. _____

3. Discuss the need for both real and nominal forecasts:

    A. Real: _____

    B. Nominal: _____

4. Identify the five-step approach managers should employ to combine nominal and real forecasts.

    A. _____

    B. _____

    C. _____

    D. _____

    E. _____

5. Identify four issues associated with emerging markets that impact enterprise DCF valuation.

    A. _____

    B. _____

    C. _____

    D. _____

6. The effect of differential growth on revenues can be examined by splitting revenue growth into real and inflation components. Forecast revenue so that Revenue (year 2) = Revenue (year 1) × (1 + Real growth rate) × (1 + Inflation rate). Here are the assumptions for the analysis:

	Year				
Assumptions	**1**	**2**	**3**	**4**	**5 Onward**
Real revenue growth		5%	5%	5%	1%
EBITDA/revenue	0.30	0.30	0.30	0.30	0.30
Tax rate	0.50	0.50	0.50	0.50	0.50
Depreciation/net PPE (begin of year)	0.20	0.20	0.20	0.20	0.20
Net PPE (end of year)/revenues	0.40	0.40	0.40	0.40	0.40
Working capital/revenues	0.20	0.20	0.20	0.20	0.20
Inflation rate	20%	50%	20%	10%	5%
Inflation index	1.00	1.50	1.80	1.98	

A. Project NOPLAT, invested capital, and free cash flow on an unadjusted deflated basis for 15 years, by deflating revenues only:

Proforma Financials	Unadjusted Deflated Forecasts				Continuing Value
	1	2	3	4	15
Revenues	$1,000				
EBITDA					
Depreciation	——	——	——	——	——
Operating income					
Tax	——	——	——	——	——
NOPLAT	══	══	══	══	══
Working capital					
NPPE (begin of year)	$ 350				
Less: Depreciation					
Plus: Capex	——	——	——	——	——
Net PPE (end of year)	——	——	——	——	——
Invested capital	══	══	══	══	══
EBITDA					
Less: Tax					
Less: Capex					
Less: Working capital increase	——	——	——	——	——
Free cash flow	══	══	══		══

B. Project NOPLAT, invested capital, and free cash flow on a nominal basis for 15 years:

Proforma Financials	Nominal Forecasts				Continuing Value
	1	2	3	4	15
Revenues	$1,000				
EBITDA					
Depreciation	——	——	——	——	——
Operating income					
Tax	——	——	——	——	——
NOPLAT	══	══	══	══	══
Working capital					
NPPE (begin of year)	$ 350				
Less: Depreciation					
Plus: Capex	——	——	——	——	——
Net PPE (end of year)	——	——	——	——	——
Invested capital	══	══	══	══	══
EBITDA					
Less: Tax					
Less: Capex					
Less: Working capital monetary result and increase	——	——	——		——
Free cash flow	══	══	══		══

C. Project NOPLAT, invested capital, and free cash flow for 15 years:

Proforma Financials	Real Forecasts				Continuing Value
	1	2	3	4	15
Revenues	$1,000				
EBITDA					
Depreciation	——	——	——	——	——
Operating income					
Tax	——	——	——	——	——
NOPLAT					
Working capital					
NPPE (begin of year)	$ 350				
Less: Depreciation					
Plus: Capex	——	——	——	——	——
Net PPE (end of year)	——	——	——	——	——
Invested capital					
EBITDA					
Less: Tax					
Less: Capex					
Less: Working capital monetary result and increase	——	——	——	——	——
Free cash flow					

D. Compare the approaches using the following results template:

	Forecasts				Continuing Value
Results	1	2	3	4	15
Real NOPLAT *					
Real free cash flow *					
Invested capital/revenue					
ROIC pretax					
ROIC posttax					

* For nominal forecast: Deflate NOPLAT and free cash at inflation point index.

7. Given the free cash flow developed previously, compare discounted cash flow. Use 8 percent real cost of capital:

A. The continuing value nominal weighted cost of capital is _____.

B. The continuing value nominal growth rate is _____.

C. Calculate unadjusted deflated forecast DCF:

	Forecasts					Continuing Value
Results	1	2	3	4	5–14	15
Real WACC	___	___	___	___	[ ]	___
Unadjusted deflated free cash flow	___	___	___	___	[ ]	___
Continuing value	[ ]				[ ]	___
Discount factor	___	___	___	___	[ ]	___
PV of free cash flow	___	___	___	___	___	___
Unadjusted deflated DCF	___					

Free cash flow for years 1 to 15 is to be taken directly from the free cash flow forecast from Question 6. Continuing value is discounted by the real WACC net of the real growth rate in perpetuity.

D. Calculate nominal forecast DCF:

Results	Forecasts					Continuing Value
	1	2	3	4	5–14	15
Nominal WACC	___	___	___	___	[____]	___
Nominal free cash flow	___	___	___	___		___
Continuing value	[_____]					___
Discount factor	___	___	___	___		___
PV of free cash flow	___	___	___	___	___	___
Nominal DCF	___					

E. Calculate real forecast DCF:

Results	Forecasts					Continuing Value
	1	2	3	4	5–14	15
Real WACC	___	___	___	___	[____]	___
Real free cash flow	___	___	___	___		___
Continuing value	[_____]					___
Discount factor	___	___	___	___		___
PV of free cash flow	___	___	___	___	___	___
Real DCF	___					

F. Comment on the results:

_____

_____

_____

23

Valuing High-Growth Companies

The best way to value high-growth companies (those whose organic revenue growth exceeds 15 percent annually) is with a classic DCF valuation, buttressed by microeconomic fundamentals and probability weighted scenarios. Although scenario-based DCF may sound suspiciously retro, it works where other methods fail, since the elements of economics and finance apply even in uncharted territory.

1. Explain how the process of valuing a high-growth company differs from valuing an established company? In what way would valuing a high-growth firm be similar to valuing an established firm that has recently hired a new chief executive officer?

---

2. How could scenario analysis be employed to gain a better understanding of the value drivers embedded in a high-growth firm?

---

3. Identify the key issues an analyst should consider when valuing start-up companies. How might an analyst resolve these issues?

_____

_____

_____

4. Identify similarities and differences of business-to-consumer to business-to-business valuations in terms of value drivers, controlling growth, economic scenarios.

Area	B2C	B2B
Drivers		
Controlling growth		
Scenarios		

24

Valuing Cyclical Companies

In Chapter 24, we explore the valuation dynamics particular to cyclical companies. A cyclical company is one whose earnings demonstrate a repeating pattern of significant increases and decreases. The earnings of such companies fluctuate because of large changes in the prices of their products or changes in volume. Volatile earnings introduce additional complexity into the valuation process as historical performance must be assessed in context of the cycle. A decline in performance does not necessarily indicate a long-term negative trend, but rather a shift to a different part of the cycle.

1. List two reasons why cyclical firms (e.g., airlines, paper, steel, chemicals) are difficult to value:

   A. _____

   B. _____

2. Outline the steps for calculating cyclical firm value:

   A. _____

   B. _____

   C. _____

   D. _____

3. Follow the steps to value PGG. Here is data for the past few years:

	2001	2002	2003	2004	2005
Financial data input					
Current assets	$ 2,595	$ 2,615	$ 2,916	$ 2,645	$ 4,559
Current liabilities	1,764	2,490	3,020	2,648	4,191
Debt in current liabilities	0	0	0	0	0
Long-term debt	7,052	6,817	6,460	6,928	8,831
Total assets	12,335	12,818	12,950	12,700	16,897
Capital expenditures	1,503	1,564	892	951	2,609
Change in deferred taxes	10	14	100	38	73
Sales	14,313	13,024	13,094	13,342	17,977
Operating expenses	9,794	9,798	10,209	10,231	13,333
General expenses	1,406	1,475	1,296	1,204	1,670
Depreciation	984	996	1,017	997	1,013
Investment income	—	—	128	24	355
Interest expense	432	459	465	443	495
Miscellaneous income, net	—	(5)	(60)	(15)	—
Income taxes	679	135	106	202	705
Beta	1.33	1.33	1.33	1.33	1.33

A. First, produce invested capital, NOPLAT, free cash flow, and economic profit statements as well as return on invested capital (ROIC)
value tree to examine the PGG's cyclical character. Develop a normal
scenario value for GP. Here are templates for the statements and
ROIC value tree:

	2001	2002	2003	2004	2005
Invested capital statement					
Working capital					
Long-term assets					
Operating invested capital					
Net investment					
Debt					
Equity					
NOPLAT statement					
Sales					
Operating expenses					
General expenses					
Depreciation					
EBIT					
Taxes on EBIT					
Change in deferred taxes					
NOPLAT					
Provision for income taxes					
Tax shield on interest expense					
Tax on investment income					
Tax on non-operating income					
Taxes on EBIT					
Net income statement					
Sales					
Operating expenses					
General expenses					
Depreciation					
EBIT					
Investment income					
Investment expense					
Miscellaneous, net					
Earnings before taxes					
Income taxes					
Net income (before extra items)					
Tax rate					

(continued)

	2001	2002	2003	2004	2005
Reconciliation to net income statement					
Net income					
Add: Increase in deferred taxes	_____	_____	_____	_____	_____
Adjusted net income					
Add: Interest expense after tax	_____	_____	_____	_____	_____
Income available to investors					
Less: Interest income after tax					
Less: Non-operating income after tax	_____	_____	_____	_____	_____
NOPLAT	══════	══════	══════	══════	══════
ROIC tree					
ROIC	_____	_____	_____	_____	_____
= (1 − EBIT cash tax rate) × Pretax ROIC	_____	_____	_____	_____	_____
= EBIT/Sales × Sales/Invested capital	_____	_____	_____	_____	_____
EBIT/Sales = 1 − (Operating expenses/Sales + General expenses/Sales + Depreciation/Sales)	_____	_____	_____	_____	_____
Sales/Invested capital = 1 /(Operating working capital/Sales + Long-term operating assets/Sales)	_____	_____	_____	_____	_____
Change in deferred tax/Sales					
Free cash flow statement					
NOPLAT					
Depreciation	_____	_____	_____	_____	_____
Gross cash flow	══════	══════	══════	══════	══════

(continued)

	2001	2002	2003	2004	2005
Increase in operating working capital					
Capital expenditures	___	___	___	___	
Gross investment	___	___	___	___	
Free cash flow	___	___	___	___	
Non-operating cash flow	___	___	___	___	
Cash flow available to investors	___	___	___	___	
Cost of capital					
Beta					
Debt/invested capital					
Equity/invested capital					
Cost of debt					
Cost of equity					
Weighted average cost of capital					
Economic profit					
NOPLAT					
Capital charge	___	___	___	___	
Economic profit	___	___	___	___	

Value the normal scenario using the following templates:

	Average 2001–2005	F 2006	F 2007	F 2008	CV 2009
Working capital					
Net fixed assets					
Invested capital					
Net investment					
Debt					
Equity					
Sales growth					
Net sales					
Operating expense					
General expense					
Depreciation					
EBIT					
Change in deferred tax					
Net operating profit less adjusted tax					
Net investment					
Free cash flow					
Cost of capital					
Economic profit					
Beta					
Unlevered beta					
PV factors					
PV short term forecast					
Continuing value					
PV continuing value					
Market value of asset					
Debt					
Market value of equity					
Number of shares					
Stock price					

	Average 2001–2005	F 2006	F 2007	F 2008	CV 2009
	Sum				
PV economic profit 1–3					
Continuing value					
PV continuing value					
Invested capital					
Market value of asset					
ROIC					
D/IC					
Eq/IC					
Tax rate					
Interest rate					
Growth (Investment/ Capital)					
Investment rate (Growth/ROIC)					
EBIT/Sales					
Sales/IC					
WC/Sales					
NFAOA/Sales					
Operating expenses/Sales					
SG&A/Sales					
Deprecation/Sales					
Change in deferred tax/Sales					

B. Formulate a new-trend scenario using the following pulp and paper industry data:

Sales growth (5-year)	6%
Beta	1.01
Operating expense/sales	70%

Value the new-trend scenario using the following templates:

	Average 2001–2005	F 2006	F 2007	F 2008	CV 2009
Working capital	243,400				
Net fixed assets	10,474,000				
Invested capital	10,717,400				
Net investment					
Debt	7,217,600				
Equity	3,499,800				
Sales growth					
Net sales	14,350,000				
Operating expense					
General expense					
Depreciation					
EBIT					
Taxes on EBIT					
Change in deferred tax					
Net operating profit less adjusted tax					
Net investment					
Free cash flow					
Cost of capital					
Economic profit					
Beta	1.37				
Unlevered beta	0.6043				
PV factors	1				

PV sums

PV short term forecast	
Continuing value	
PV continuing value	
Market value of asset	

Market value

Number of shares
Stock price

	Average 2001–2005	F 2006	F 2007	F 2008	CV 2009
	Sum				
PV economic profit 1–3					
Continuing value					
PV continuing value					
Invested capital					
Market value of asset					
ROIC	6.36%				
D/IC	67.34%				
Eq/IC	32.66%				
Tax rate	38.71%				
Interest rate	6.83%				
Growth (investment/ capital)					
Investment rate (Gwh/ROIC)					
EBIT/sales					
Sales/IC					
WC/sales	1.6962%				
NFAOA/sales	72.9895%				
Operating expenses/sales	74.3763%				
SG&A/sales	9.8272%				
Deprecation/sales	6.9784%				
Change in deferred tax/sales	0.391%				

C. Use a framework such as the value hexagon to explain the valuation scenarios and their effect on GP's value.

D. Assign probabilities, weight each scenario's stock price, and produce a combined valuation.

Scenario	Probability (%)	Value
Normal		
New trend		

25

Valuing Financial Institutions

1. The following is a simplified balance sheet for a bank with associated yields:

Community Bank, Inc.			Rate (%)
Assets	Cash reserves	$ 150	
	Loans	850	11
	Total assets	$1,000	
Liabilities	Deposits	$ 950	4
	Equity	50	
	Total liabilities	$1,000	

Assume a 7 percent intercompany interest rate on reserves for the spread model. Also assume a 40 percent tax rate.

A. Calculate net income with the income model:

Interest income
Interest expense
Other expenses
Net profit before taxes
Taxes
Net income

B. Calculate net income with the spread model:

Loan spread
Deposit spread
Equity spread
Reserve debt
Expenses
Net profit before taxes
Taxes
Net income

C. Compare the two methods:

_____

_____

_____

_____

_____

2. Develop a bank valuation forecast narrative:

The model starts with a forecast of _____ growth. Loans are then determined by a _____ ratio. _____ reserves work from a cash reserve-to-total deposit ratio, reflecting Federal Reserve policy. Premises, equipment, and other assets are required to support deposits directly and loans indirectly. Investments are related to cash reserves. Given a level of _____, a managerially determined _____ to total asset relationship is determined. Federal Funds Purchased balances_____. _____ balances the balance sheet. Noninterest income and expense are related to deposit size. Forecasts of interest rates drive the _____, term borrowing, investment, and _____ rates.

3. The following is a very simplified version of Neighborhood Bank System's balance sheet, income statement, and average rates for 2005. Value Neighborhood Bank System, Inc., using the equity cash flow method. Depreciation is $1.434 million for 2005. Neighborhood Bank System, Inc.'s equity beta is 1.20.

Income Statement 2005	Amount	Rate (%)
Interest income	66.919	8.11
Less: Interest expense	(25.221)	3.52
Net interest income	41.698	4.59
Plus: Other income	5.120	
Less: Other expenses	(26.498)	
Net profit before tax	20.320	
Less: Taxes	(7.721)	38.00
Net income	12.598	

Balance Sheet 2005	Amount	Rate (%)
Cash reserves	32.411	
Investment securities	378.520	6.93
Net loans	446.135	9.12
Net premises, other assets	25.526	
Less: Provision for credit losses	(6.281)	
Total assets	876.311	
Interest-bearing deposits	552.892	3.29
Non-interest-bearing deposits	98.587	
Other short-term liabilities	6.102	
Federal funds purchased	57.300	4.00
Term borrowings	05.550	4.49
Liabilities	820.431	
Shareholders' equity	55.880	13.48
Total	876.311	

Neighborhood Banking System, Inc. Key Ratios and Assumptions

	Historical	Explicit Forecast Period			CV Period
	2005	2006	2007	2008	2009
Loan/deposit	68.48%	72.00%	71.00%	70.00%	69.00%
Other liabilities/total assets	0.70%	0.70%	0.70%	0.70%	0.70%
Term borrowing/total assets	12.04%	12.00%	12.00%	12.00%	12.00%
Liabilities/total assets	93.62%	94.00%	94.00%	94.00%	93.00%
Cash reserves/investment	8.56%	8.50%	8.50%	8.50%	8.50%
Cash reserves/deposits	4.97%	5.00%	5.00%	5.00%	5.00%
Deposit growth	15.00%	15.00%	12.00%	10.00%	0.00%
Provision for loan loss/net loans	1.41%	1.40%	1.40%	1.40%	1.40%
Premises, other assets/deposits	3.92%	3.92%	3.92%	3.92%	3.92%
Other income/deposits	0.79%	0.75%	0.75%	0.75%	0.75%
Other expenses/deposits	4.07%	4.10%	4.10%	4.10%	4.10%
Depreciation/net premises	5.62%	5.62%	5.62%	5.62%	5.62%
Beta	1.20	1.30	1.40	1.40	1.30

A. Calculate net income using the following template on page 85.

B. Calculate the balance sheet using the template on page 86.

Income statement

| | Explicit Forecast Period | | | | | | CV Period | |
| | 2005 | | 2006 | | 2007 | | 2008 | | 2009 | |
	Amount	Rate	Amount	Rate	Amount	Rate	Amount	Rate	Amount	Rate
Interest income										
Less: Interest expense										
Net interest income										
Plus: Other income										
Less: Other expenses										
Net profit before tax										
Less: Taxes										
Net income										

Balance Sheet

	2005		Explicit Forecast Period 2006		2007		2008		CV Period 2009	
	Amount	Rate	Amount	Rate	Amount	Rate	Amount	Rate	Amount	Rate
Cash reserves										
Investment securities										
Net loans										
Net premises, other assets										
Less: Provision for credit losses										
Total assets										
Interest bearing deposits										
Non-interest-bearing deposits										
Other short-term liabilities										
Federal funds purchased										
Term borrowings										
Liabilities										
Shareholders' equity										
Total										

C. Calculate equity cash flows and the value to equity holders using following template:

Equity Cash Flow and Value

| | 2005 | Explicit Forecast Period | | | CV Period |
		2006	2007	2008	2009
Net income					
Plus: Depreciation					
Less: Increase in assets					
Plus: Increase in liabilities					
Equity cash flow					
Present value factor					
PV equity cash flows					
PV continuing value					
Market value of equity					
Number of shares	5.987				
Stock price					

4. Identify the value drivers embedded in the equity cash flow model unique to industrial companies and financial companies:

Value Drivers

Industrial Companies	Financial Companies
A.	A.
B.	B.

5. Define *duration*. Why is duration important both for understanding a financial institution's risk and for analyzing performance?

_____

_____

_____

6. Define the term *reserves* as it relates to a life insurance company's liability section of the balance sheet. In what way is a life insurance company's reserve position similar to a company's accumulated pension obligation?

_____

_____

_____

Part Two

Answers

1

Why Maximize Value?

1. B

2. B, C, E, F, H

3. C

4. B, C

5. B, C

6. B, D

7. A, B, D

8. A. Growth in earnings.
   B. Declines in interest rates.
   C. Mega-capitalization stocks associated with the *Internet bubble*.

9. A. Internet bubble.
   B. LBO bubble.

10. Countries with the lowest returns have been those that experienced the most economic upheaval, often with long periods of high inflation, civil

strife, or defeat in war. These markets have relatively few companies listed on stock markets, compared with the United States and United Kingdom. In addition to higher returns in the United States, P/E and market-to-book ratios have been significantly higher for the U.S. market when compared with Europe and key Asian markets. Performance differences explain much of the difference in valuation, particularly in the case of return on capital. U.S. companies consistently earn higher returns on capital than companies in Europe and Asia.

2

The Value Manager

1. D

2. A. Focus on long-term cash flow rather than quarter-to-quarter earnings, take stock of value creation within the company and identify various restructuring activities.

   B. Judge businesses by returns above opportunity costs, rather than size, prestige, and other emotional issues.

   C. Instill value creating culture within the company to generate continuum of value creating (including elimination of value destroying) activities.

3. B

4. A. Sensitivity analysis was performed.

   B. EG's business units were compared to similar companies.

   C. Corporate overhead was examined and opportunities to reduce costs were reviewed.

5.

	Strength	Weakness
Consumerco	Dominant market and strong brand	Limited growth
Woodco	Plan for common sales and marketing	High operating costs and uneven performance
Foodco	Good brand, aggressive capital base	Small player

6. A. EG lags its peers and the market.

   B. Strong brands not fully exploited.

   C. Probably a good break-up play, due to uneven performance across businesses.

7. D

8.

Component	Products	Results
Current valuation	EG performance from shareholder perspective	Woodco acquisition accompanied by price downturn.
		Consumerco growing at inflation rate only.
		Consumerco cash flow subsidizes Woodco and Foodco.
		High capital requirements for Foodco erodes earnings growth.
		Analysts constantly revise EG forecasts downward.
As is value	DCF	Historical value below market value.
		Foodco value is less than the invested capital, focused on growth over return.
		Consumerco's cash flow comprises most of EG's value.
		Headquarter's costs are significant drag on value.

(continued)

Component	Products	Results
Value with internal improvements	Key value drivers, comparable firm and business system analysis	Consumerco holding prices down, not investing in R&D, sensitive to sales, lack of productivity—sales staff, high CGS.
		Woodco to focus on higher margins, less growth; remain in mass production market.
		Foodco has no advantages in highly competitive market, trim to profitable locations only, franchise to decrease costs.
		Reduce overhead (50%).
Value with external Improvements	Four scenario break-up analysis: sale to strategic buyer, floatation, MBO, liquidation	Simple breakup based on comparable P/Es, M/B would not outperform current market value.
		Consumerco is natural buyout given high cash flows.
		Foodco's RE holdings make it a partial liquidation candidate.
		Sell consumer finance portfolio.
		Due to consolidation, Woodco would not likely attract buyer due to the risk of reconstructing its many components.
		EG takeover candidate due to Consumerco's CFs.
New growth opportunities	L-T alternatives	Put acquisition and alternative growth alternatives on agenda.
		Incubate new businesses.
		Promote l-t growth imperative with each restructuring alternative.
Value from financial engineering	Liability alternatives	Use stable cash flows to support higher debt levels.
		Find ways to return cash flow to shareholders; repurchase shares, special dividends.

9. C

10. A. Focus performance on value creation.
    B. Develop value-based performance targets and measurement system.
    C. Restructure EG's compensation system to emphasize the creation of shareholder value.
    D. Communicate value to investors.
    E. Reshape CFO role.

11. B

12. D

3

Fundamental Principles of
Value Creation

1. B, C, D

2. D

3. B

4. C

5. B, C, D

6. A. Install forward-looking performance measures.

   B. Align managers to value performance through incentives.

7. A. Earn returns in excess of opportunity cost of capital.

   B. Growth can create value only when excess returns are earned.

   C. Select strategies that maximize the intrinsic present value of future economic profit or cash flow.

   D. Market expectations might not be unbiased estimates of intrinsic value.

   E. Shareholder returns depend on changes in their expectations of future performance rather than on actual performance.

8. Fred's objective should be to maximize shareholder value that is attainted via the maximization of economic profit over the long term, not ROIC. Consider an extreme example: Most investors would prefer $200,000 (a 20 percent return on $1 million of capital) to $500 (a 50 percent on $1,000 of capital).

9. Begin with the basic valuation model:

	A	B
IR = .6	$200,000 = \dfrac{5,000(1-.6)}{.1-(.15\times.6)}$	$28,571 + \dfrac{5,000(1-.6)}{.1-(.05\times.6)}$
IR = .4	$75,000 = \dfrac{5,000(1-.4)}{.1-(.15\times.4)}$	$37,500 = \dfrac{5,000(1-.4)}{.1-(.05\times.4)}$

When ROIC is greater than WACC, value is maximized by reinvesting all free cash flows into the firm. When ROIC is less than WACC, value is maximized by reinvesting no free cash flows into the firm. The value drivers, thus, dictate when and if reinvestment should occur.

4

Do Fundamentals Really Drive the Stock Market?

1. Market efficiency may be defined by stating: The market price of an asset is exactly equal to the intrinsic value (the present value of the cash flows) of the asset; there are no positive or negative net present value opportunities. In a perfectly efficient market, both price and value change only when new information reaches the market. When new information reaches the market, there is an immediate and simultaneous adjustment to both intrinsic value and market price: The faster the adjustment, the more efficient the market; the slower the adjustment, the less efficient the market.

2. Overall, share price levels have reflected economic fundamentals very well over long periods of time. Marketwide price deviations from fundamentals occur, but are clearly the exception. Managers can safely assume that markets are reflecting intrinsic value and are long-term efficient. The market assigns value to companies (such as biotech or high-tech) without any near-term earnings. This indicates that the market takes a long-term view. In case of pharmaceutical companies, the market exhibits a strong price reaction to pipeline announcements for which there is no near-term earnings impact at all. Product and pipeline development is a much better indicator of the long-term growth and profitability of pharmaceutical companies than short-term earnings. Overall, share price levels have reflected economic fundamentals quite well over the past four decades. The principles that drove share prices in the 1960s still

remain valid today, despite significant economic ups and downs, industrial restructurings, and technological and other changes.

3. The basic economic law that directs market behavior is: Value is driven
   by returns on capital and growth. The U.S. and U.K. stock markets have
   been fairly priced and have oscillated around their intrinsic price-
   earnings ratios as estimated from long-term returns on capital and
   growth. Marketwide price deviations from these intrinsic price-earnings
   ratios have been rare over the past 45 years. In the late 1970s, prices were
   too low as investors were obsessed with high short-term inflation rates.
   In the late 1990s, market prices reached excessive levels that could not be
   justified by the underlying economic fundamentals. However, such marketwide price deviations are typically short lived: Over the past four
   decades, the market corrected itself within a few years to price levels
   consistent with economic fundamentals.

4. A. Irrational investor behavior. "Irrational" investors do not process all
      available information correctly when forming expectations on the
      stock's future performance. Studies of the investment behavior of pro-
      fessional fund managers and analysts show various forms of such ir-
      rationality.

   B. Systematic patterns of behavior across different investors. If individ-
      ual investors decided to buy or sell without consulting economic fun-
      damentals, the impact on share prices would be limited. Only when
      they behave irrationally also in a systematic way should persistent
      price deviations occur. Behavioral finance theory argues that patterns
      of overconfidence, overreaction, and overrepresentation are common
      to many investors, and such groups can be large enough to prevent a
      company's share price—at least for some stocks, some of the time—
      from reflecting underlying economic fundamentals.

   C. Limits to arbitrage in financial markets. If there are enough rational
      investors in a market, and there are no barriers to arbitrage, system-
      atic patterns of irrational behavior can be exploited, and they will not
      have lasting effects on market valuations. In reality, such arbitrage is
      not always possible. Transaction costs and risks are involved in set-
      ting up and running the arbitrage positions.

5. A. Issuing additional share capital at times when the stock market is at-
      taching too high a value to the company's shares relative to intrinsic
      value.

   B. Repurchasing company shares when the stock market underprices
      relative to the intrinsic value.

C. Paying for acquisitions with shares instead of cash when the stock market overprices the shares relative to intrinsic value.

D. Divesting particular businesses at times when trading and transaction multiples in that sector are higher than can be justified by underlying fundamentals.

5

Frameworks for Valuation

1. A. Free cash flow measured annually (or another appropriate period).

   B. Discount each cash flow by a rate of return commensurate with the riskiness of the cash flows (WACC or k_u).

   C. Sum up the discounted cash flows to generate an enterprise value. In the simple case of free cash flow growing at a constant rate:

   $$\text{Value}_0 = \frac{\text{FCF}_1}{\text{WACC} - g}$$

2. A. Free cash flow is "net operating profit less adjusted taxes," NOPLAT, minus net investment.

   B. Net investment is the amount of new capital beyond replacement capital and thus represents the growth in invested capital.

   C. The investment rate is the percentage of NOPLAT that the firm decides to invest in new capital.

3. A. Value the company's operations by discounting free cash flow from operations at the weighted average cost of capital.

   B. Value nonoperating assets, such as excess marketable securities, nonconsolidated subsidiaries, and other equity investments. Combining the value of operating assets and nonoperating assets leads to enterprise value.

   C. Identify and value all nonequity financial claims against the company's assets. Nonequity financial claims include (among others) fixed- and floating-rate debt, pension shortfalls, employee options, and preferred stock.

    D. Subtract the value of nonequity financial claims from enterprise value to determine the value of common stock. To determine share price, divide equity value by the number of shares outstanding.

4. A. NOPLAT

    B. WACC

    C. Invested Capital

    D. Growth rate

The economic profit model discounts the period-by-period forecasted economic profit by the weighted-average, risk-adjusted, cost of capital. In the simple case of economic profit growing at a constant rate:

$$\text{Value}_0 = \text{Invested capital}_0 + \frac{\text{Economic profit}_1}{\text{WACC} - g}$$

$$\begin{aligned}\text{Economic profit} &= \text{Invested capital} \times (\text{ROIC} - \text{WACC})\\ &= \text{NOPLAT} - (\text{Invested capital} \times \text{WACC})\end{aligned}$$

    1. Since the economic profit valuation was derived directly from the free cash flow model (see Appendix B for the proof of equivalence), any valuation based on discounted economic profits should be identical to enterprise DCF. However, to assure equivalence with DCF, you must measure invested capital as of the end of the previous year.

    2. Use the same invested capital number for both economic profit and ROIC.

5. A. Grow capital at an ROIC greater than the cost of capital.

    B. Decrease capital to lower the capital base, while maintaining NOPLAT at current levels.

    C. Lower the weighted average, risk adjusted, cost of capital, WACC, by adjusting the company's financial structure.

6. This analysis follows ideas introduced as long ago as 1920 (GM residual income model) and more recently with Bennett Stewart's Quest for Value who labels the three firms as X, Y, Z.

    Consider three prototypical firms. Firm X's NOPLAT grows at a 10 percent rate per year. It reinvests 100 percent of NOPLAT per year so that its capital growth is 10 percent per year, just like NOPLAT's growth. The increase in NOPLAT per increase in capital is a return of 10 percent on a NOPLAT base of $1,000.

Then there is firm Y whose NOPLAT growth on $1,000 is also 10 percent. However, firm Y reinvests 80 percent of its NOPLAT into capital. Its rate of return is higher at 12.5 percent. Firm Y grows NOPLAT at the same rate as firm X, but uses less capital to do so; firm Y should be more profitable. Firm Y also generates more free cash flow, as measured by NOPLAT minus investment.

Finally, there is firm Z. This firm also earns a base NOPLAT of $1,000. But this firm, unlike X or Y reinvests 200 percent of NOPLAT in the capital base. Firm Z generates a negative free cash flow of $1,000 − [2 × 1,000] = −$1,000. This means that any dividends or interest and principal to be paid out must be financed each year.

	X	Y	Z
ROIC	10.0%	12.5%	12.5%
WACC	10.0%	10.0%	10.0%
Growth	10.0%	10.0%	25.0%
IR	100.0%	80.0%	200.0%
NOPLAT	1,000	1,000	1,000
Net investment	1,000	800	2,000
FCF	0	200	−1,000
NOPLAT increase	100.0	100.0	250.0
ROIC new capital	10.0%	12.5%	12.5%
EP new capital	0.0	20.0	50.0

Most bankers might prefer firm Y, with firm X second, and firm Z to be bankrupted. Let's further suppose that all three firms are perceived by the markets to have the same expected level of risk at a 10 percent cost of capital. Let firm Z earn the same ROIC as firm Y (i.e., 12.5 percent).

Firm Z grows more rapidly than X or Y at 25 percent (12.5 percent × 200 percent = ROIC × Investment/NOPLAT). For firm Z, the increase in NOPLAT is really at the 25 percent rate, so that an extra 250 is earned on an extra $2,000 of capital (12.5 percent return). Thus, firm Z's aggressive capital spending campaign will fuel even higher levels of NOPLAT growth. Profitability is high, just like firm Y. But so is the firm's growth and the growth in NOPLAT, something that firm Y does not achieve.

Which firm provides greater value added? The clear winner is firm Z. The curve ball is firm Z's willingness to fuel higher NOPLAT with additions to capacity, the long run and fundamental fix.

To summarize: Firm X generates 0 free cash flow by investing all of its earnings in a mediocre operation resulting in no value added. Firm Y generates part of its earnings in a mediocre enterprise, keeps some free cash flow and does add some value. Firm Z generates negative free cash flow by investing more than its earnings in a superior enterprise and thereby adds much more value than either X or Y. Firm Z plans to pump more money into excellent projects on a regular, predictable basis.

7. The steps in a valuation include:

   A. Analyze historical performance. Gather together a set of appropriate comparable firms. Calculate NOPLAT, invested capital, and value drivers. Integrate into this analysis a perspective that includes a business system, strategic, and industry analysis.

   B. Forecast performance. Use the current industry and firm strategic position to construct probable scenarios for various future competitive positions. Forecast line items. Check for completeness, consistency, and parsimony.

   C. Estimate the cost of capital. Develop target market value weights for each capital category. Estimate the costs of equity and nonequity financing with careful attention to using as objective a set of criteria and modeling as possible.

   D. Estimate continuing value. Consider the explicit forecast horizon, appropriate valuation techniques, and key parameters. Discount to the present using the cost of capital.

   E. Calculate and interpret results. Finish the valuation by tying together the explicit forecast and continuing value discounts. Interpret results within the strategic change envisioned for the firm and the concomitant decisions that need to be taken to maximize value.

Thinking about Return
on Invested Capital
and Growth

1. A. Price Premium (Branding). In commodity markets, companies are price takers. Price takers must sell at the market price to generate business. Alternatively, a price setter has control over the price it charges. To enable price setting, a company cannot sell a commoditized product.

   B. Cost Competitiveness. A second driver of high ROIC is a company's ability to sell products and services at a lower cost than the competition.

   C. Capital Efficiency. Even if profits per unit (or transaction) are small, a company can generate significant value by selling more products per dollar of invested capital than its competition.

7

Analyzing Historical Performance

1. A. Starting points: Return on invested capital (ROIC) and the weighted average cost of capital (WACC). ROIC measures the firm's ability to yield net results to all stakeholders, irrespective of financing arrangements. The return investors require to be compensated for the risk of the firm's business operations is measured by WACC. The difference between ROIC and WACC measures the per currency unit of capital results of a firm's operations. This spread is the economic profit yield of the firm. When multiplied by the amount of beginning (or average) capital, economic profit is measured.

   B. Ultimate goals: To help managers and investors understand when the firm is creating value. (the analysis is not simply a calculation of ROIC or WACC measures, but their combination in an economic profit calculation. When ROIC exceeds WACC, managers are returning positive economic profits. When ROIC equals or falls short of investors' risk adjusted expectations, there are economic losses. Economic profit adds market value and creates an excess demand for the company's stock).

2. A. Convert the company's financial statements to reflect economic, rather than accounting performance, creating such new terms as net operating profit less adjusted taxes (NOPLAT), invested capital, and free cash flow (FCF).

B. Measure and analyze the company's return on invested capital (ROIC) and economic profit to evaluate the company's ability to create value.

C. Break down revenue growth into its four components: organic revenue growth, currency effects, acquisitions, and accounting changes.

D. Assess the company's liquidity and evaluate its capital structure to determine whether the company has the financial resources to conduct business and make short and long-term investments.

3. A. Using the Dupont system, ROIC, like any ratio, can be decomposed into several underlying components. The result is a tree of ROIC determinants. At the top is ROIC. At the second level are pretax ROIC and EBIT cash tax rate (CTR). On the next level are asset turnover and operating income margin. Further levels can be constructed by decomposing operating income margin and asset to sales turns into their components, and so on.

ROIC is first stripped of tax considerations into a pretax ROIC:

$$\text{Pretax ROIC} = \frac{\text{NOPLAT}}{[1 - \text{EBIT cash tax rate}]}$$

where, from the NOPLAT statement, EBIT CTR equals:

$$\text{CTR} = \frac{\text{Taxes on EBIT} + \text{Change in deferred taxes}}{\text{EBIT}}$$

B. Tax considerations in this analysis are relegated to a different category than are operational experiences. Tax rates, and the extent to which they can be effectively managed, must be compared across firms in the firm's industry universe.

Pretax ROIC can be further decomposed into:

$$\text{Pretax ROIC} = \frac{\text{EBIT}}{\text{Sales}} \times \frac{\text{Sales}}{\text{Invested capital}}$$

EBIT/sales, the operating margin or operating return on sales, measures the way sales converts into after expenses income. Within-period operating efficiency is measured by this ratio. Sales/invested capital measures how effective capital is in producing sales. More sales for every dollar of long-run operating capital shows an effective use of capital. Higher capital turns coupled with a highly efficient operation, in terms of a high operating margin, produces high levels of ROIC for a given CTR. In turn, a poor ROIC can be produced by three significant factors: high tax rates, inefficient operations, and ineffective capital.

EBIT/sales in turn can be decomposed into the various cost components of operating income:

$$\frac{EBIT}{Sales} = 1 - \frac{Expense}{Sales}$$

where

$$\frac{Expense}{Sales} = \frac{COGS}{Sales} + \frac{SG\&A}{Sales} + \frac{Dep}{Sales}$$

where COGS is cost of goods sold, SG&A is sales, general, and administrative expenses, and Dep is depreciation. While depreciation is a noncash expense, it does attempt to represent the user cost of expended capital during the period of operation. In this sense, capital is an unexpended cost to be maintained within the context of the going concern of the perpetual firm.

C. Capital effectiveness, measured by sales/invested capital can also be decomposed:

$$\frac{Sales}{Capital} = \frac{1}{\left[\frac{WC}{Sales} + \frac{NFA}{Sales} + \frac{OA}{Sales} \right]}$$

where WC is working capital, NFA is net fixed assets, and OA is net other operating assets. Lower values of these ratios indicated increased effectiveness of the components of the invested capital portfolio as they contribute to sales.

4. Here is the beginning of the historical analysis:

	2004	2005
Invested Capital Statement		
Working capital	154	117
Long-term assets	1,430	1,411
Operating invested capital	1,584	1,528
Debt	507	447
Equity and equity equivalents	1,077	1,081
NOPLAT Statement		
Sales	4,056	4,192
Operating expenses	(3,307)	(3,408)
General expenses	(562)	(528)
Depreciation	(139)	(136)
EBIT	48	120
Taxes on EBIT	(31)	(53)
Change in deferred taxes	(29)	(20)
NOPLAT	(12)	47
Provision for income taxes	(7)	41
Tax shield on interest expense	25	13
Tax on investment income	(3)	(3)
Tax on non-operating income	16	2
Taxes on EBIT	31	53

Invested capital can be viewed from an operating and financing perspective. On the operating side is operating working capital and long-run operating capital net of accumulated depreciation. Operating working capital is operating current assets (not marketable securities) net of noninterest bearing current liabilities (NIBCLs). On the financing side is debt currently due plus long-term debt. The remainder is equity, computed as a residual between invested capital and debt. This equity amount includes total booked equity plus equity equivalents, such as deferred taxes.

NOPLAT equals sales minus operating costs minus operating taxes. The accounting statement of net income provides a total provision for income taxes. This provision includes tax deductions for interest payments and taxes and deductions for non-operating income. Adjusting for these items, we get taxes on EBIT. One further adjustment is required due to the mismatching of accounting tax treatments and the actual treatment due to accelerated depreciation schemes for tax deductibility of depreciation. This last adjustment is contained in the changes to the virtual perpetual loan the tax authorities give a firm—deferred taxes.

5. The net income statement and its reconciliation to NOPLAT:

	2004	2005
Net Income Statement		
Sales	4,056	4,192
Operating expenses	(3,307)	(3,408)
General expenses	(562)	(528)
Depreciation	(139)	(136)
EBIT	48	120
Investment income	5	6
Interest expense	(39)	(30)
Miscellaneous income, net	(25)	(4)
Earnings before taxes	(11)	92
Income taxes	7	(41)
Net income (before extra items)	(4)	51
Reconciliation to Net Income Statement		
Net income	(4)	51
Add: Increase in deferred taxes	(29)	(20)
Adjusted net income	(33)	31
Add: Interest expense after tax	14	17
Income available to investors	(19)	48
Less: Investment income after tax	(2)	(3)
Less: Non-operating income after tax	9	2
NOPLAT	(12)	47

The primary utility of this exercise is to be sure that the NOPLAT statement is complete and consistent with the data. It is complete because all of the relevant cost, tax, and operating data included in the accounting net income statement is also included for operations in the NOPLAT statement. It is consistent with the net income statement through the reconciliation process. That process primarily derives from the cash tax treatment.

6. Here is the value driver tree:

	2004	2005
ROIC Tree		
ROIC	−0.7%	3.0%
= (1 − EBIT cash tax rate)	−24.1%	38.8%
× Pretax ROIC	3.0%	7.9%
= EBIT/Sales	1.2%	2.9%
× Sales/Invested capital	2.56	2.74
EBIT/Sales = 1 − (Operating expenses/Sales	81.5%	81.3%
+ General expenses/Sales	13.9%	12.6%
+ Depreciation/Sales)	3.4%	3.2%
Sales/Invested capital		
= 1/(Operating working capital/Sales	3.8%	2.8%
+ Long-term operating assets/Sales)	35.3%	33.7%

The ROIC in 2004 is negative. The tree shows that the low pretax ROIC derives from a low operating margin of 1.2 percent and an ineffective capital usage of $2.56 sales for every $1 of capital invested in operations. The low operating margin derives from high expense-to-sales ratios. The low capital effectiveness derives from high capital to sales ratios.

The situation improves from 2004 to 2005 with an improvement in ROIC to 7 percent. This is due both to improvements in operations (lower costs, increased operational efficiency) and in capital utilization (less assets relative to sales).

7. The free cash flow statement:

	2005
Free Cash Flow Statement	
NOPLAT	47
Depreciation	136
Gross cash flow	183
Increase in operating working capital	(37)
Capital expenditures	117
Gross investment	80
Free cash flow	103
After tax non-operating cash flow	1
Cash flow available to investors	104

Free cash flow is the difference between NOPLAT and net investment. Net investment in turn is the gross investment net of depreciation. Investment derives from changes in operating working capital and capital expenditures. Total cash flow available to investors includes free cash flow from operations plus non-operating income.

8. Economic profit is the difference between operating earnings, NOPLAT, and the return expected by investors for the level of risk perceived.

The capital charge is the 11.1 percent weighted average cost of capital times the amount of capital. This is a period in the life of the firm that is value destroying:

	2004
NOPLAT	47
Capital charge	(175.8)
Economic profit	(−128.8)

9. Compare the free cash flow and economic profit statements. Both measures begin with NOPLAT, operating earnings generated by operating capital. Free cash flow measures the residual cash from operations after

increases in new capital (beyond replacement capital) have been deducted from operating earnings. Conversely, economic profit measures the residual value from operations after a risk adjusted opportunity cost has been deducted from operating earnings.

Free cash flow is useful for determining the funds use and need during a period's operations. Economic profit is useful for determining the ability of a period's operations to contribute to the increase or decrease in the overall value of the enterprise.

For BMI, free cash flow is positive. This might make bondholders happy, since their cash sensitive position would require prompt and complete contractual payments on outstanding debt. However, for all of the excess cash produced, there is not enough operating income to pay the investors what they expect given their perceptions of risk. BMI is value detracting, perhaps, because it does not have profitable opportunities in which to invest.

8

Forecasting Performance

1. A. Prepare and analyze historical financials. Before forecasting future financials, you must understand past financials.

   B. Build the revenue forecast. Almost every line item will rely directly or indirectly on revenue. You can estimate future revenue by using either a top-down (market-based) or bottom-up (customer-based) approach. Forecasts should be consistent with historical economy-wide evidence on growth.

   C. Forecast the income statement. Use the appropriate economic drivers to forecast operating expenses, depreciation, interest income, interest expense, and reported taxes.

   D. Forecast the balance sheet: invested capital and nonoperating assets. On the balance sheet, forecast operating working capital; net property, plant, and equipment; goodwill; and nonoperating assets.

   E. Forecast the balance sheet: investor funds. Complete the balance sheet by computing retained earnings and forecasting other equity accounts. Use excess cash and/or new debt to balance the balance sheet.

   F. Calculate ROIC and FCF. Calculate ROIC to assure forecasts are consistent with economic principles, industry dynamics, and the company's ability to compete. To complete the forecast, calculate free cash flow as the basis for valuation. Future FCF should be calculated the same way as historical FCF.

2. The evaluation of strategic position itself asks at least the following six questions:

Buyers	Who are they? What are their preferences? What pricing and product practices will meet their expectations? Increasing ROIC derives from enhanced revenues, less charge backs for returned and poor quality product, and reasonably designed customer satisfaction.
Suppliers	Again, who are they? How can they best serve the firm in its mission to serve the firm's customers and clients? Increasing ROIC and lower WACC derives from lower, efficient, and more productive and effective cost and asset structures. Lower WACC derives from higher financial quality, lower perceived risks from financial capital suppliers, due to lower perceived volatility and greater ability to manage uncertainty.
Technology	What is the cycle of innovation in the industry, the rate of turnover of generations of capital, the ability of the firm to innovate in well-planned research and development? Higher ROIC and lower WACC derive from the firm's short run ability to react to incursions in its technological base and obsolescence as technology turns over from generation to generation. More R&D means lower-cost production and products that meet the changing expectations of customers.
Government	What are the cycles of regulation, deregulation, and re-regulation in the industry? How do these regulatory movements impact production, choice of capital, choice of where to raise capital, vendor quality, liability with stakeholders, and choice of customer market segments? Each of these items impacts: (1) the firm's ability to charge a market-based price based on customer type, (2) the firm's ability to influence operating margins, and ultimately (3) the ability of investors to earn a rate of return that exceeds the risk-adjusted cost of capital.
New entrants	What are the threats, barriers to entry, ability to re-engineer new technology, and entrepreneurial availability in the industry? This question directly impacts the ability of the firm to maintain its positive ROIC over WACC, in other words, its quasi-monopolistic position. Relatively low barriers to entry can be produced by skewed regulatory systems, for example, that favor small over larger businesses. In the long run, a financial forecast must recognize the positive probability of handing over the long-run asset base produced by current thinking and technology to new entrants. In this case, ROIC will tend to WACC and even fall below WACC at which point the firm goes out of its current business and into another.
Substitute products/services	A similar set of questions and logic obtains for this inquiry as for new entrants. As IBM found out with its RISC technology, even a competing product can be found within a firm's multidivisional structure.

High value added occurs with high ROIC and low WACC. High ROIC occurs with higher operational efficiency (seller), more effective capital (seller, technology), achieving lower costs than the competition (substitute products, new entrants), and providing superior value to the customer (buyer).

3.

Customer segmentation	Estimates the potential market share, growth of sales and ability to maintain and grow markets. The company segments customers and products by various attributes, then associates those attributes with the various core competencies of the firm to provide goods and services.
Business system	Analysis provides the core competencies and abilities of the firm to meet customer expectations. Issues such as time-to-market, access to sources of material and labor, cycle time, packaging, and distribution channels are combined to highlight the competitive advantages and disadvantages the firm possesses in its industry.
Industry structure analysis	Industry structure provides insight into the cycle of feed forward and feedback networks at work in the industry analysis of buyer, seller, government, technology, new entrants, and substitute product attributes. This component of the analysis provides the dynamic interrelationships among various industry players.

4.

$$\text{Enterprise Value} = \sum_{i=1}^{\infty} \frac{\text{FCF}_1}{(1+\text{WACC})^1} + \frac{\text{FCF}_2}{(1+\text{WACC})^2} + \ldots + \frac{\text{FCF}_n}{(1+\text{WACC})^n}$$

Since enterprise value is based upon the PV of free cash flows to the company we note that an impact to either free cash flows or to the discount rate will impact value. In this case we know that the discount rate:

$$\text{WACC} + \frac{D}{V} k_d (1-t) + \frac{E}{V} k_e$$

is comprised of the average of the after-tax cost of debt and the cost of equity. Since the cost of debt is not equal to the cost of equity, any change in the weighting of these components will typically change WACC, thus the value of the firm will change.

5. The CO scenario is maintenance of past operating results and represents, for management and management's communication to the investment community, the effects of a noninnovative scenario. The AG scenario is the one that management could hope for if all conditions are right, in-

Aggressive	Historic 2004	Forecast 2005	2006	2007
WC	193.000	270.113	378.158	529.421
NFA	246.000	345.744	484.042	677.658
IC	439.000	615.857	862.199	1,207.079
Net investment		176.857	246.343	344.880
Debt	314.000	400.307	560.429	784.601
Equity	125.000	215.550	301.770	422.478
Sales growth		40.00%	40.00%	40.00%
Net sales	1,029.000	1,440.600	2,016.840	2,823.576
Operating expense		(1,066.044)	(1,472.293)	(2,061.210)
SG&A		(230.496)	(322.694)	(451.772)
Depreciation		(36.015)	(50.421)	(70.589)
Operating income		108.045	171.431	240.004
Taxes on EBIT		(43.218)	(68.573)	(96.002)
Change in deferred tax		2.795	3.913	5.478
NOPLAT		67.622	106.772	149.480
ROIC		10.98%	12.38%	12.38%
D/IC		65.00%	65.00%	65.00%
Eq/IC		35.00%	35.00%	35.00%
Tax rate	-21.62%	40.00%	40.00%	40.00%
Interest rate	5.10%	6.00%	7.00%	7.00%
Growth (investment/ capital)		40.29%	40.00%	40.00%
Investment rate (growth/ ROIC)		366.90%	323.01%	323.01%
EBIT/sales		7.5000%	8.5000%	8.5000%
Sales/IC		2.3392	2.3392	2.3392
WC/Sales	18.7561%	18.7500%	18.7500%	18.7500%
NFA/Sales	23.9067%	24.0000%	24.0000%	24.0000%
Operating expense/sales	74.3440%	74.0000%	73.0000%	73.0000%
SG&A/sales	18.5617%	16.0000%	16.0000%	16.0000%
Depreciation/sales	2.5267%	2.5000%	2.5000%	2.5000%
Change in deferred tax/sales	0.194%	0.194%	0.194%	0.194%
Free cash flow		(109.235)	(139.571)	(195.400)

cluding those not in management's power. Implicit in the success that an AG scenario represents is management's willingness to put resources to value-adding activities when they occur, either by design, or as a result of market conditions.

Conservative	Historic 2004	Forecast 2005	2006	2007
WC	193.000	231.525	277.830	333.396
NFA	246.000	296.352	355.622	426.747
IC	439.000	527.877	633.452	760.143
Net investment		88.877	105.575	126.690
Debt	314.000	343.120	411.744	494.093
Equity	125.000	184.757	221.708	266.050
Sales growth		20.00%	20.00%	20.00%
Net sales	1,029.000	1,234.800	1,481.760	1,778.112
Operating expense		(926.100)	(1,111.320)	(1,333.584)
SG&A		(229.673)	(275.607)	(330.729)
Depreciation		(31.200)	(37.440)	(44.928)
Operating income		47.828	57.393	68.871
Taxes on EBIT		(19.131)	(22.957)	(27.548)
Change in deferred tax		2.396	2.875	3.450
NOPLAT		31.092	37.310	44.772
ROIC		5.89%	5.89%	5.89%
D/IC		65.00%	65.00%	65.00%
Eq/IC		35.00%	35.00%	35.00%
Tax rate	−21.62%	40.00%	40.00%	40.00%
Interest rate	5.10%	6.00%	7.00%	7.00%
Growth (investment/ capital)		20.25%	20.00%	20.00%
Investment rate (growth/ ROIC)		343.72%	339.56%	339.56%
EBIT/sales		3.8733%	3.8733%	3.8733%
Sales/IC		2.3392	2.3392	2.3392
WC/sales	18.7561%	18.7500%	18.7500%	18.7500%
NFA/sales	23.9067%	24.0000%	24.0000%	24.0000%
Operating expense/sales	74.3440%	75.0000%	75.0000%	75.0000%
SG&A/sales	18.5617%	18.6000%	18.6000%	18.6000%
Depreciation/sales	2.5267%	2.5267%	2.5267%	2.5267%
Change in deferred tax/sales	0.194%	0.194%	0.194%	0.194%
Free cash flow		(57.785)	(68.265)	(81.918)

6.

Driver	Low Growth: Conservative	High Growth: Aggressive
Operating expenses/sales	74%	74%, 73%, 73%
SGA/sales	19%	16%
Growth	20%	40%
Other	Ratios constant	Ratios constant

In each there are four columns. The first is the last available historical year, 2004, followed by, in this case, three forecast years, 2005, 2006, 2007. A simplified invested capital statement precedes the calculate of the forecasted net investment, or change in invested capital useful in the subsequent free cash flow calculation. Next comes the NOPLAT statement. Items in boxes are input to the forecasting process. Finally, ratios, forecasted and derived, and a free cash flow forecast are provided.

Since this is a sales driven forecast, historical sales starts the forecast. Sales growth is projected over the forecast period. Next year's sales is equal to this year's, times one, plus the projected growth rate for sales over the period. This year's expenses equal the year's forecasted sales times the appropriate forecasted expense ratio. Similarly, working capital and long run asset ratios are used to project forecasted invested capital items from this year's forecasted sales.

Forecasts of debt to invested capital ratios and projected debt interest rates will be used in the cost of capital.

Tax rate forecasts are used both for cost of capital studies and the forecast of NOPLAT. Forecasted changes in deferred taxes to sales are used in the NOPLAT calculation.

A number of derived results can attest to the effect of these particular scenarios on the firm. ROIC is a constant 10.56 percent, below the 2004 high of 13.5 percent, due primarily to the positive 40 percent tax rate. However, EBIT to sales is vastly improved from 4.6 percent to 7.2 percent, not on the backs of line workers directly involved with producing revenues, but on low quality and value detracting overhead activities with a lower general expense-to-sales ratio. Caution must be exercised in achieving the low general expense ratio of 16 percent in that truly value-detracting activities be identified and culled from the high-quality, revenue, and productivity enhancing overheads.

The AG scenario forecasts higher ROIC, better operations and no change in effective use of capital. Free cash flow is increasingly negative. The CO scenario posts the poorest performance, with low ROIC, operations, and capital ratios. Capital is required as sales rise by 20 percent per year. Cash flow is negative with net investment exceeding NOPLAT.

9

Estimating
Continuing Value

1. A. Length of the explicit forecast affects the company's value.

   B. Confusion concerning the relationship of continuing value to the length of time a company is forecast to earn returns on invested capital greater than its cost of capital—its competitive advantage period.

   C. Some analysts incorrectly infer that a large continuing value relative to the company's total value implies that value creation occurs primarily after the explicit forecast period.

2. A. The level of NOPLAT should be based on a normalized level of revenues and sustainable margin and ROIC. The normalized level of revenues should reflect the midpoint of its business cycle and cycle average profit margins.

   B. The expected rate of return on new invested capital (RONIC) should be consistent with expected competitive conditions. Economic theory suggests that competition will eventually eliminate abnormal returns, so for many companies, set RONIC equal to WACC. However, for companies with sustainable competitive advantages (e.g., brands and patents), you might set RONIC equal to the return the company is forecast to earn during later years of the explicit forecast period.

   C. Few companies can be expected to grow faster than the economy for long periods. The best estimate is probably the expected long-term rate of consumption growth for the industry's products, plus inflation. Sensitivity analyses also are useful for understanding how the growth rate affects continuing-value estimates.

D. The weighted average cost of capital should incorporate a sustainable capital structure and an underlying estimate of business risk consistent with expected industry conditions.

3.

Assumptions	Years 1–3 (%)	Years 4+ (%)
ROIC	18	11
Growth	20	7
WACC	14	12

3-Year Horizon	1	2	3	CV Base
NOPLAT	10.00	12.00	14.40	15.41
Depreciation	2.50	3.00	3.60	
Gross cash flow	12.50	15.00	18.00	
Gross investment	(13.61)	(16.33)	(19.60)	
Free cash flow	(1.11)	(1.33)	(1.60)	
Discount factor	0.8772	0.7695	0.6750	
Present value FCF	(0.97)	(1.03)	(1.08)	
PV FCF 1–3	(3.08)			
PV CV	75.64			
Total value	72.56			

5-Year Horizon	1	2	3	4	5	CV Base
NOPLAT	10.00	12.00	14.40	15.41	16.49	17.64
Depreciation	2.50	3.00	3.60	3.85	4.12	
Gross cash flow	12.50	15.00	18.00	19.26	20.61	
Gross investment	(13.61)	(16.33)	(19.60)	(13.66)	(14.61)	
Free cash flow	(1.11)	(1.33)	(1.60)	5.60	6.00	
Discount factor	0.8772	0.7695	0.6750	0.6027	0.5381	
Present value FCF	(0.97)	(1.03)	(1.08)	3.38	3.23	
PV FCF 1–3 5	3.53					
PV CV	69.03					
Total value	72.56					

Value is the same for each horizon. This is only because the calculation for free cash flow, and its associated present value, is consistent for the two cases. For the three-year horizon, and the first three years of the five-year horizon, the calculations are identical. The first two years of the three-year horizon CV base and years 4 and 5 of the five-year horizon are also identical. This can be noted by looking at the free cash flows for the explicit forecast period in the five-year horizon. For years 1 to 3, the negative free cash flows dive from gross investment that exceeds gross cash flow. This in turn results from a growth rate that exceeds the ability of those assets to return a profit during those years. Years 4 and 5 yield free cash flows that are positive. In those years of the explicit forecast, growth is less than return on new investment, which returns a surplus cash flow, just as it does, by assumption, for the CV base year and thereon into the 75 plus years that effectively comprise the growing perpetuity.

All that has happened in the valuation is a different split on the same value. For the short-term forecast, the explicit forecast period produces (3.08) in present value with the rest of the 75.64 of continuing base value. The longer run horizon split is a positive 3.53 for the explicit forecast plus a commensurately lower CV base value of 63.03. Both add up to the same amount, 72.56 because both are effectively using the same cash flow streams.

4. Assume a two-period explicit forecast horizon, weighted average cost of capital w, return on invested capital r, net operating profit after adjusted taxes N, invested capital C, capital growth rate g. We let date 0 be the beginning of the first period and the date at which valuation occurs; dates 1 and 2 are the ends of periods 1 and 2, respectively; date 3 is the end of the first period in the continuing base time frame. The value, V_0, of the entity is the present value of free cash flow:

$$V_0 = \frac{\left[N_1 - (C_1 - C_0)\right]}{(1+w)^1} + \frac{\left[N_2 - (C_2 - C_1)\right]}{(1+w)^2} + \frac{\left[\dfrac{N_3 - (C_3 - C_2)}{w - g}\right]}{(1+w)^2}$$

Where the first two terms are the present value of NOPLAT less net investment, the change in invested capital from the end of the previous period to the end of the current period, and the third term is the present value of the growing free cash flow perpetuity.

To construct an equivalent economic profit version of the free cash flow valuation, add and subtract wC_0 in the numerator of the first term, and similarly add and subtract wC_1 in the numerator of the second term. This operation is algebraically neutral so that we still have the same free cash flow valuation as when we started. The resulting, and really not so tedious algebra, gives us:

$$V_0 = C_0 + \frac{\left(N_1 - wC_0\right)}{(1+w)^1} - \frac{C_1}{(1+w)^1}$$

$$+ \frac{C_1}{(1+w)^1} + \frac{\left(N_2 - wC_1\right)}{(1+w)^2} - \frac{C_2}{(1+w)^2}$$

$$+ \frac{\left[\frac{\left(N_3 - C_3 + C_2\right)}{(w-g)}\right]}{(1+w)^2}$$

Now take the $-C_2/(1+w)^2$ in the second line, multiply it by one, that is, by $(w-g)/(w-g)$, and incorporate it into the growing perpetuity term in the third line. In the mean time let terms in C_1 add up to zero in the first and second lines. After all of this we have:

$$V_0 = C_0 + \frac{\left(N_1 - wC_0\right)}{(1+w)^1} + \frac{\left(N_2 - wC_1\right)}{(1+w)^2} + \frac{\left[\frac{N_3 - C_3 + C_2}{(w-g)} - \frac{C_2(w-g)}{(w-g)}\right]}{(1+w)^2}$$

The third line is the present value of the continuing value base. We multiply C_2 through by $(w-g)$ and rearrange terms to get the equivalent term:

$$\frac{\left\{\frac{\left(N_3 - wC_2\right)}{(w-g)} + \frac{\left[gC_2 - \left(C_3 - C_2\right)\right]}{(w-g)}\right\}}{(1+w)^2}$$

We realize that:

$$C_3 = C_2 + gC_2$$

or

$$gC_2 = C_3 - C_2$$

so that the numerator of the second term in the brackets equals zero. Finally, we have shown that the original free cash flow valuation V_0 is:

$$V_0 = C_0 + \frac{\left(N_1 - wC_0\right)}{(1+w)^1} + \frac{\left(N_2 - wC_1\right)}{(1+w)^2} + \frac{\left[\dfrac{\left(N_3 - wC_2\right)}{(w - g)}\right]}{(1+w)^2}$$

The value of the entity using free cash flows is the present value of the free cash flows in each explicit forecast period plus the present value of the growing free cash flow perpetuity in the continuing base period. The value of the entity using economic profit is the initial capital base plus the present value of economic profit for the explicit forecast period plus the present value of the growing economic profit perpetuity during the continuing base period.

5. A numerical example will illustrate the algebraic demonstration and will also show that the valuation is robust to different assumptions about the weighted average cost of capital between the explicit forecast period and the continuing base period.

Net Investment$_t$ is $(g_t/\text{ROIC}_t)\text{NOPLAT}_t$ and NOPLAT$_{t+1}$ is NOPLAT$_t$ $(1 + g)$. Beginning capital plus net investment equals new capital.

Assumptions	Years 1–3 (%)	Years 4+ (%)
ROIC	18.00	15.75
Growth	20.00	5.00
WACC	14.00	12.00

3-Year Horizon	1	2	3	CV Base
NOPLAT	10.00	12.00	14.40	15.12
Net investment	(11.11)	(13.33)	(16.00)	
Free cash flow	(1.11)	(1.33)	(1.60)	
Beginning IC	55.56	66.67	80.00	
Net investment	11.11	13.33	16.00	
New IC	66.67	80.00	96.00	
NOPLAT	10.00	12.00	14.40	
Capital charge	(7.78)	(9.33)	(11.20)	
Economic profit	2.22	2.67	3.20	
Discount factor	0.8772	0.7695	0.6750	
Present value FCF	(0.97)	(1.03)	(1.08)	
Present value EP	1.95	2.05	2.16	
PV FCF 1–3	(3.08)			
PV CV FCF	99.51			
Total value	96.43			
PV EP 1–3	6.16			
PV CV	34.71			
IC	55.56			
Total value	96.43			

In this example, economic profit is positive while free cash flow is negative during the explicit forecast period. The firm is value adding while at the same time requiring net new investment in excess of operating earnings. A critical assumption for the operation of the model is that the ROIC (15.75 percent) for the continuing base period must be consistent with continuing base period NOPLAT and the level of capital at the end of the explicit forecast period (equivalently the beginning of the continuing base period).

The free cash flow model shows the firm how much funding is generating or is needed during forecast periods. This representation would be certainly useful to the corporate treasurer and the maintenance of long-run goals for the firm's money desk and bank cash management relationships. The economic profit valuation shows the firm how much value is gained or lost during forecast periods. The primary audience for this representation would be banks, and other contractual claimants on the firm's ability to generate earnings.

If value-based management is founded on value-adding activities, then the economic profit representation motivates the judgment that negative free cash flows during the explicit forecast period are fine as long as they add value in the future. Already the future has been discounted by markets. The weighted average cost of capital represents risk premia assessed by the market regarding the ability of the entity to add forward value. This representation is useful for value-based managers who are required by agency relationships with stakeholders and specifically shareholders to add value or at least minimize the occurrence of value detracting activities. The economic profit profile of the firm summarizes the short-term, within period, effects of long-run value maximizing activities and strategies. The primary audiences for the economic profit representation would be shareholders and managers whose compensation is value-based and other managers who need to see how their achievement of short-run targets affect long-run value added.

6. In this example, IMT is forecasted to have a 10 percent to 15 percent to 20 percent sales growth over the explicit forecast period. NOPLAT for the continuing value base is forecasted from the desired 4 percent rate of growth for the firm into the long run. ROIC is then calculated at the CV NOPLAT as a percent of 2002 invested capital. The investment rate of 35.15 percent then results in positive free cash flow.

IMT Valuation	H 2001	F 2002	F 2003	F 2004	CV 2005
Working capital	193.000	212.231	244.066	292.879	—
Net fixed assets	246.000	271.656	312.404	374.885	—
Invested capital	439.000	483.887	556.470	667.764	694.475
Net investment		44.887	72.583	111.294	26.711
Debt	314.000	338.721	378.400	434.047	451.409
Equity	125.000	145.166	178.071	233.718	243.066
Sales growth		10.00%	15.00%	20.00%	
Net sales	1,029.000	1,131.900	1,301.685	1,562.022	
Operating expenses		(848.925)	(963.247)	(1,124.656)	
General expenses		(210.533)	(242.113)	(281.164)	
Depreciation		(28.600)	(32.890)	(39.468)	
Earnings before interest and tax		43.842	63.435	116.735	
Taxes on EBIT		(17.537)	(25.374)	(46.694)	
Change in deferred tax		2.196	2.525	3.030	
Net operating profit less adj tax		28.501	40.586	73.071	75.994
ROIC	13.48%	6.49%	8.39%	13.13%	11.38%
D/IC	71.53%	70.00%	68.00%	65.00%	65.00%
Eq/IC	28.47%	30.00%	32.00%	35.00%	35.00%
Tax rate	−21.62%	40.00%	40.00%	40.00%	40.00%
Interest rate	5.10%	6.00%	7.00%	7.00%	5.00%
Growth (investment/ capital)		10.22%	15.00%	20.00%	4.00%
Investment rate (Gwh/ROIC)		157.49%	178.84%	152.31%	35.15%
EBIT/sales		3.8733%	4.8733%	7.4733%	
Sales/IC		2.5784	2.6901	2.8070	
WC/sales	18.7561%	18.7500%	18.7500%	18.7500%	
NFAOA/sales	23.9067%	24.0000%	24.0000%	24.0000%	
Operating expenses/sales	74.3440%	75.0000%	74.0000%	72.0000%	74.0000%
SG&A/sales	18.5617%	18.6000%	18.6000%	18.0000%	18.6000%
Depreciation/sales	2.5267%	2.5267%	2.5267%	2.5267%	2.5267%
Change in deferred tax/sales	0.194%	0.194%	0.194%	0.194%	0.194%
Free cash flow		(16.386)	(31.997)	(38.223)	49.283
Cost of capital		7.82%	8.27%	8.33%	7.55%
Economic profit		(5.812)	0.558	26.738	25.603
Beta	1.73	1.942	1.821	1.665	1.665
Unlevered beta	0.4266	0.5827	0.5827	0.5827	0.5827
PV factors	1	0.927504	0.856641	0.790798	

(continued)

IMT Valuation	H 2001	F 2002	F 2003	F 2004	CV 2005
	PV Sums				
PV short term forecast	(72.835)	(15.198)	(27.410)	(30.227)	
Continuing value				1,389.751	
PV continuing value	1,099.012				
Value of IMT	1,026.177				
Debt	(314.000)				
Market value of equity	712.177				
Number of shares	33.7				
Stock price	21.13				
PV EP 1–3	16.232	(5.391)	0.478	21.145	
Continuing value				721.986	
PV CV	570.945				
IC	439.000				
Value of IMT	1,026.177				

With 33.7 million outstanding shares, IMT can rationalize a $21.13 share value using these numbers. Notice the path of free cash flow versus economic profit. Free cash flow is naturally negative during the expansion envisioned in the explicit forecast period from 2000 through 2003. At the same time, economic profit starts negative but by 2001 becomes positive and lays the foundation for long-run positive value addition in the continuing value base period.

10

Estimating the Cost of Capital

1. A. WACC must include the opportunity costs from *all* sources of capital: debt, preferred equity, common equity, since free cash flow is available to all investors, who expect compensation for the risks they take.

   B. WACC must weight each security's required return by its target market based weight, not by its historical book value.

   C. WACC must be computed after corporate taxes (since free cash flow is calculated in after-tax terms).

   D. WACC must be denominated in the same currency as free cash flow.

   E. WACC must be denominated in nominal terms when cash flows are stated in nominal terms.

2. A. Raw regressions should use at least 60 data points (e.g., five years of monthly returns). Rolling betas should be graphed to examine any systematic changes in a stock's risk.

   B. Raw regressions should be based on monthly returns. Using shorter return periods, such as daily and weekly returns, leads to systematic biases.

   C. Company stock returns should be regressed against a value weighted, well-diversified portfolio, such as the S&P 500 or MSCI World Index.

3.

$$\text{WACC} = \frac{D}{V} k_d (1-t) + \frac{E}{V} k_e$$

4. A. Estimate the target weights for each layer of capital.

   B. Estimate the after-tax cost of debt capital.

   C. Estimate the cost of equity capital.

   D. Compute the weighted average cost for each layer of capital financing.

5. A. Estimate current market value of the capital structure of the company.

   B. Review capital structure of comparable companies.

   C. Review management's approach to financing and its implications for a target capital structure.

6.

Bond 1	0	1	2
Interest		−100	−100
Principal	1,000		−1,000
Net cash flow	1,000	−100	−1,100
Yield to maturity	10%		

Bond 2	0	1	2
Interest		−100	−50
Principal		−500	−500
Net cash flow	1,000	−600	−550
Yield to maturity	10%		

7.

Bond 1	0	1	2
Interest received			
Interest paid		−100	−100
Taxes		40	40
Principal	1,000		−1,000
Net cash flow	1,000	−60	−1,060
Yield to maturity	6%		

Bond 2	0	1	2
Interest received			50
Interest paid		−100	−100
Taxes		40	20
Principal	1,000	−500	−500
Net cash flow	1,000	−560	−530
Yield to maturity	9%		

8.

$$\text{WACC} = \frac{D}{V} k_d (1-t) + \frac{E}{V} k_e : \left[\frac{40}{100} \times .073 \times (1-.40) \right] + \left[\frac{60}{100} .113 \right] = .0853 = 8.53\%$$

9. A. $k_d = .073 + .0075 = .0805$

B. $E(R_i) = r_f + ß_i [E(Rm) - r_f]: .1236 = .06 + ß_i [.113 - .06]: .0636 = ß_i [.053]:$
  $ß_i = 1.2$

C.

$$ß_u = \frac{ß_L}{\left[1 + \frac{D}{E} \times (1-t) \right]} : ß_u = \frac{1.2}{\left[1 + \frac{.2}{.8}(1-.4) \right]} = 1.04$$

D.

$$ß_L = ß_u \times \left[1 + \frac{D}{E} \times (1-t) \right] : ß_L = 1.04 \left[1 + \frac{.5}{.5} \times (1-.4) \right] = 1.66$$

E. $E(R_i) = r_f + ß_i [E(Rm) - r_f]: 06 + 1.66 [.113 - .06] = .15$

F.

$$\text{WACC} = \frac{D}{V} k_d (1-t) + \frac{E}{V} k_e : [.5 \times .0805 \times (1-.4)] + [.5 \times .15] = .099 = 9.9\%$$

11

Calculating and
Interpreting Results

1. A. Discount free cash flows.

    B. Discount continuing value.

    C. Calculate the value of operations.

2. A. Calculate and test. Discount the free cash flow, or economic profit, from explicit forecast and continuing value-base periods. Add investing capital to the economic profit value. Add in the value of nonoperating net income and excess marketable securities, as well as the value of any nonrelated businesses. Subtract the value of debt and other nonequity forms of capital to get the market value of equity. Finally, divide the market value of equity by the number of average outstanding shares to derive a stock price. Perform this exercise for each scenario.

    B. Interpret the results in the decision context. For each scenario, identify the operative assumptions and their relationship to the various components of the valuation. The margin for error in each scenario can be deduced by changing key value drivers and noticing their effect on the entity value generated in a scenario. If the decision is to set a target debt to invested capital ratio, then a scenario with a 65 percent debt-to-capital ratio can be examined by changing capital growth, annual sales growth, operational ratios, and the like to see how sensitive value is to this decision. Be sure to examine alternative scenarios that might occur if interactive elements in the environment occur, such as competitive retaliation. The evaluation of additional scenarios might uncover further questions not already anticipated.

3. A. Debt such as bonds, short-term and long-term bank loans.

   B. Debt equivalents such as operating leases, pensions, specific types of provisions, preferred stock, and contingent liabilities (e.g., outstanding claims from litigation).

   C. Hybrid claims such as employee stock options and convertible bonds.

   D. Minority interests.

4.

Ownership Position <20%	Ownership Position 20%–50%
For equity stakes below 20 percent, the parent company is assumed to have no influence. The equity holdings are shown at historical cost on the parent's balance sheet. The parent's portion of the subsidiary's dividends is included below EBIT on the income statement and does not affect free cash flow.	For equity stakes between 20 percent and 50 percent, the parent company is assumed to have influence but not control over the subsidiary. The equity holding in the subsidiary is reported in the parent balance sheet at the investment's historical cost plus profits and additional investment, less dividends received. The parent company's portion of the subsidiary's profits is shown below EBIT on the income statement and does not affect free cash flow.

5. A. Verifying valuation results by conducting a consistency check to confirm that outcomes are consistent with assumptions made.

   B. Conduct a sensitivity analysis to assure results are robust under alternative assumptions.

   C. Evaluate the plausibility of the results by comparing calculated value to market price.

6. First, the valuation of the enterprise provides a manager a baseline or comparison to evaluate the impact of investment opportunities. Further, computing the value of a corporation provides the executive a deeper understanding and appreciation of both what drives the value of the firm and how actions taken impact stock price. The purpose of valuing a company is often to guide a management decision related to acquisition, divestiture, or adoption of internal strategic initiatives. Since most of these decisions involve uncertainty and risk, a more thorough understanding of the drivers of value becomes critical to the success of an executive.

12

Using Multiples
for Valuation

1. When supplemental valuation analysis is careful and well reasoned, relative valuation models not only provide a useful check of DCF forecasts but also provide critical insights into value drivers within a given industry. Thus, analyzing a set of multiples to better understand how a company is valued relative to its peers provides significant value to the analyst.

2. A. Choose comparables with similar prospects for ROIC and growth.

   B. Use multiples based on forward-looking estimates.

   C. Use enterprise-value multiples based on EBITA to mitigate problems with capital structure and one-time gains and losses.

   D. Adjust the enterprise-value multiple for nonoperating items, such as excess cash, operating leases, employee stock options, and pension expenses.

3.

Relative Valuation Model	DCF Valuation Model
$$\text{Value}_0 = \dfrac{\text{EBITA}(1-t)\left[1-\left(\dfrac{g}{\text{ROIC}}\right)\right]}{\text{WACC}-g}$$	$$\text{Value}_0 = \sum_{t=1}^{\infty} \dfrac{FCF_t}{(1+\text{WACC})^t}$$
Creating a multiple:	Assuming growth is constant:
$$\dfrac{\text{Value}}{\text{EBITA}} = \dfrac{(1-t)\left[1-\left(\dfrac{g}{\text{ROIC}}\right)\right]}{\text{WACC}-g}$$	$$\text{Value}_0 = \dfrac{FCF}{\text{WACC}-g}$$

Relative valuation models normalize market-based values by some measure, such as earnings. By applying one company's earnings multiple onto another's net income, you can estimate the second company's value. The downside of this methodology is that it implicitly assumes both firms have identical financial characteristics, such as incremental return on invested capital and growth. Conversely, discounted cash flow (DCF) models provide the flexibility for modeling any financial characteristics. DCF models, however, are only as good as the forecasts they rely on. By using a multiples analysis in conjunction with DCF, you can bound and assess the quality of DCF forecasts.

13

Performance Measurement

1. A. Performance—Historically, how much economic value has the company created (as measured by the company's financial statements)?

   B. Company health—How well positioned is the company to create additional economic value in the future, and what risks may prevent this value creation?

   C. Market Value—Is the company's current market value in line with its historical performance and potential economic value creation? What accounts for recent changes in its stock price?

2. The implied P/E ratio on new debt is equal to $[1/(0.072 \times (1 - 0.35))]$, or 21.4 times. As long as the company is able to repurchase shares at less than 21.4 times earnings, earnings per share will increase as net income decreases more slowly than shares outstanding. However, when a company takes on more debt, all else equal, its shares become riskier, and its cost of equity will increase, which should reduce its P/E ratio. Financial statements explicitly recognize the gains from share repurchases, and not the costs.

3. Short-term metrics are the immediate drivers of historical ROIC and growth. They are indicators of whether growth and ROIC over the short term can be sustained, or whether they will improve or decline. Medium-term metrics go beyond short-term performance by looking forward to indicate whether a company can maintain and improve its growth and ROIC over the next one to five years.

4. A. Sales productivity metrics are the drivers of recent sales growth, such as price and quantity, market share, the company's ability to charge higher prices relative to peers (or charge a premium for its product or services), salesforce productivity, and same-store sales growth versus new-store growth for a retailer.

   B. Operating cost productivity metrics are typically drivers of unit costs, such as the component costs for building an automobile or delivering a package.

   C. Capital productivity measures how well a company uses its working capital (inventories, receivables, and payables) and its property, plant, and equipment.

5. A. Commercial health metrics indicate whether the company can sustain or improve its current revenue growth. These metrics include the company's product pipeline (talent and technology to bring new products to market over the medium term), brand strength (investment in brand building), and customer satisfaction.

   B. Cost structure health measures a company's ability to manage its costs relative to competitors over three to five years.

   C. Asset structure health measures how well a company maintains and develops its assets.

6. Recall the relationship between ROIC and economic profit:

$$\text{Economic profit} = \text{Invested capital} \times (\text{ROIC} - \text{WACC}).$$

Although companies that grow with an ROIC greater than the cost of capital generate attractive EPS growth, the inverse is not true. Companies with strong EPS growth might not create value. EPS growth can be the result of either heavy investment or changes to a firm's capital structure. One disadvantage of ROIC and growth is both are measured as percentages. Neither ROIC or growth incorporate the impact of the magnitude of value creation. Thus, a small company or business unit with a 30 percent ROIC will appear more successful than a large company with a 10 percent ROIC. To overcome this problem, economic profit converts ROIC into a dollar measure, enabling the size of value creation to be incorporated into comparisons with other companies. Economic profit may also be used to measure the trade-offs between growth and ROIC.

14

Performance Management

1. A. Complete buy-in at all levels on the priority and mind-set of value creation.

   B. A clear and systematic process for both identifying and measuring the value drivers essential to the performance and health of the business.

   C. Targets for which managers feel responsible, targets must be difficult to achieve but not so unreasonable.

   D. Fact-based performance review process that balances short-term performance to long-term growth.

   E. Accountability and the process for evaluating and remunerating people.

2. Early VBM programs delivered short-term results that were not sustainable or that traded away opportunities for future growth, focused too heavily upon measurement and neglected to change the way the new measures were used. In many cases, companies developed value-based measurement systems but neglected the management of the system. Many companies neglected to link performance measurement systems to the method of compensation. The result was the creation of a system where employees had neither incentive nor direction as to where to place their focus.

3. A value driver is a lever that affects company performance in the short- or long-term thereby creating value. Metrics measure quantitatively how

the business is doing with regard to a specified value driver. Milestones measure how well the business is doing on the activities related to the value driver.

4. Corporate centers find it convenient to impose one scorecard on all business units. Although a single scorecard makes comparison of units easier, management forgoes the chance to better understand the unique drivers of value associated with each business unit. Ideally, companies should have custom-tailored scorecards cascading down in each business, so each manager can monitor the most important key value drivers.

5. If managers know the value drivers, they are able to make reasoned choices requiring a trade-off between improving one value driver and allowing another to deteriorate. This is particularly true for trade-offs between the delivery of short-term performance to activities that build the long-term health of the. Knowledge concerning value drivers enable the management team a prioritization of actions to maximize value creation.

   Moreover, without an explicit understanding of value drivers, corporate priorities, and alternatives, different members of the management team might execute the business strategy at cross purposes. Unified planning and performance management systems promote a common language—the value driver approach—that molds how to think about value creation at each level of the organization.

6. A. Develop an understanding of the economic links within the business and identify potential value drivers.

   B. Identify which value drivers have the highest priority, which have the most potential to create value.

7. The value tree is a systematic method of analytically and visually linking the business's operational elements to financial metrics and shareholder value. Each element of financial performance is decomposed into levers that business management can act upon. After creating a value tree, a series of filters is applied to define at the key value drivers for the business.

   A. Is the value driver material?

   B. How much impact can the business have on the value driver?

   C. Have unintended consequences been considered?

   D. Is the value driver sustainable?

8. The purpose of identifying an appropriate benchmark is to enable management a comparison their company's characteristics to other firms in

the industry, other units within the firm, or relative to theoretical limits. This comparison supports the identification of areas of strength and weakness. Identification of strengths and weakness enables management a more effective approach to allocate scarce resources of effort and time. Companies can identify opportunities by benchmarking performance on a particular KPI or milestone based on the following considerations:

A. External benchmarks, these compare the company's performance on a value driver with similar companies in the same industry.

B. Internal benchmarks, these compare the performance of similar units in the company.

C. Theoretical limits: Some processes or activities have physical limits on their efficiency.

D. Benchmarks against itself: These involve analyzing the historical performance of the same business over time on a particular value metric.

E. Fundamental economic analysis: This involves estimating the potential for revenue growth and ROIC based on the product market and competitive environment.

15

Creating Value through Mergers and Acquisitions

1. Set out the reasons M&A companies win or lose.

Winners	Losers
Bigger overall value	Overoptimistic market potential
Acquirer run better than acquired	Overestimate of synergies
Acquirer strength in core business	Avoidance of major problems
Link performance with incentives	Overbidding
Focus on cash flows not earnings	Chase good talent out

2. A. Do your homework concerning the restructuring opportunities within which an M&A occur.

   B. Identify and screen M&A candidates.

   C. Assess high-potential candidates in depth.

   D. Contact, court, and negotiate with candidates.

   E. Manage postmerger integration.

3. A. Leverage core business to access new customers.

   B. Capitalize on functional economies of scale.

   C. Align skills, knowledge, and technology transfer between companies.

4. A. The M&A will disrupt current business.

   B. Competitors will use M&A opportunity to woo customers away.

   C. Customers will bargain over price and quality during and after a merger.

5. A. Develop M&A database for periodic review.

   B. Apply knock-out criteria to filter candidates according to size, fit, strategy, markets, future value creation, and complementaries.

   C. Generate a short list of candidates for business unit/management review.

6.

Business System Component	Potential Synergy
Research and development	Developing new products through transferred technology
Procurement	Pooled purchasing (higher volume)/ standardizing products
Manufacturing	Eliminating overcapacity Transferring best operating practices
Sales and marketing	Cross-selling of products Using common channels
Distribution	Consolidating warehouses and truck routes
Administration	Consolidating strategy and leadership functions Exploiting economies of scale in finance/accounting and other back-office functions

7.

Issue	Resolution
Multiple business models confuse customers and employees about ability to generate value	Define and develop business model during negotiation, ready for implementation upon signing
Star performers will leave; top management will only agree abstractly about strategic direction causing confusion and conflict	Resolve uncertainty and conflict by including star performers in the process, maintain open and candid communications with all employees on frequent basis; move quickly to resolve uncertainty with practical action plans
External entities (creditors, customers, regulators, etc.) may severely criticize or hold up M&A	Maintain open communications with securities analysts, key customers

8.

Characteristic	Merger/Aquisition	Joint Venture
Overlap	High levels to gain economies of scale	Complementory with little overlap; new markets or geography
Ownership split	Uneven	Even
Decision making	Centralized strategy	Autonomous and separate decision making
Time frame	Perpetual	Contingent on meeting partner's goals

16

Creating Value
through Divestitures

1. A. Synergies or transactions between businesses.

   B. Limits on management resources of the parent company.

   C. Pricing of the asset/business.

   D. Legal, contractual, or regulatory barriers and transaction costs.

   E. Liquidity of the market for the asset/business.

2.

Transaction Approaches to Corporate Divesture	
Private	**Public**
1. *Trade sale:* Sale of part or all of a business to a strategic or a financial investor.	1. *Initial public offering:* Sale of all shares of a subsidiary to new shareholders in the stock market.
2. *Joint venture:* Combining part or all of a business with other industry players, other companies in the value chain or venture capitalists.	2. *Carve-out:* Sale of part of the shares in a subsidiary to new shareholders in the stock market.
	3. *Spin-off:* Distribution of all shares in a subsidiary to existing shareholders of the parent company.
	4. *Split-off:* An offer to existing shareholders of the parent company to exchange their shares in the parent company for shares in the subsidiary.
	5. *Tracking stock:* Separate class of parent shares that is distributed to existing shareholders of the parent company through a spin-off or sold to new shareholders through a carve-out.

Private transactions are likely to create more value than public transactions when better owners exists for the business, typically strategic buyers such as other industry players or financial buyers such as private equity. This allows a company to sell the business directly at a premium over its stand-alone value.

3. To maintain or increase the company's rate of growth, often a manager will need to harvest either cash flows generated from a mature business unit or divest a mature business in order to acquire a business unit in its initial stages of growth. The manager is not emphasizing either current EPS or growth rate, but recognizing that in a well-managed firm the firm's value is based on the present value of long-term stream of free cash flows. Divesting slow growth today for both significantly greater growth and increased future free cash flows results in increasing stock price.

4. Divestitures create value when the business unit is worth more to some other owner or in some other ownership structure. Business units can be worth more in another ownership structure because the current structure may impose unique costs on the parent and/or the business unit. Some of these costs are hidden, such as when the parent company culture is dominated by a mature business and limits innovation. In other cases, the costs are explicit, when a company lacks core skills to be an effective operator in an industry. An active portfolio management approach creates value by avoiding, eliminating, or at least minimizing these costs. Although divesting underperforming businesses avoids the direct cost of bearing the deteriorating results, divesting profitable and/or growing businesses can also benefit both the parent and the business unit.

17

Capital Structure

1. Optimal capital structure is the specific mixture of debt and equity that maximizes the value of the firm. The optimal mixture of debt and equity is that capital structure that provides the lowest WACC, thereby providing maximum shareholder value. Recall:

$$\text{Value}_0 = \text{Invested capital}_0 + \sum_{t=1}^{\infty} \frac{\text{Invested capital}_{t-1} \times (\text{ROIC}_t - \text{WACC})}{(1+\text{WACC})^t}$$

thus, a decrease in WACC leads to an increase in value—everything else held equal.

2. Academics argue that every corporation has an optimal capital structure. Most surveys among financial executives show that executives put more emphasis on preserving financial flexibility than on minimizing cost of capital. Empirical analyses have demonstrated that companies actively manage their capital structure and stay within certain leverage boundaries. Companies are much more likely to issue equity when they are overleveraged relative to this target, and much less likely when they are underleveraged. Companies typically make adjustments toward a target capital structure with one or two years' delay, rather than immediately, since that would become impractical and costly due to share price volatility and transaction costs.

   This is also the pattern we would expect to find if companies would target interest coverage: share prices are ultimately driven by future operating earnings and cash flows. If share prices rise and remain there, earnings and cash flows eventually will rise—and that is probably when companies start to increase leverage. Although leverage and coverage ratios all point in the same direction, interest coverage targets are more appropriate for setting long-term capital structure targets. One reason is that coverage measures credit quality more accurately (see the discussion of leverage and coverage in this chapter). A second reason is that leverage would be a moving target as share prices fluctuate. Coverage can be more readily applied when making long-term capital structure analyses, because it does not require any valuation estimate going forward but simply interest and EBITDA.

The final reason is that some companies are more conservative and some are more aggressive in setting capital structure targets. The more conservative the company the greater likelihood that equity based financing would be more desirable than debt financing. The more conservative the firm the less tolerance a firms has towards financial risk. Moreover, the more conservative the firm the more likely the firm will select long term financing alternatives over short-term financing alternatives.

3. The primary benefit of adding debt to the capital structure of a firm is that for any identified capital structure the interest on debt is deductible for tax purposes, whereas, dividends on equity are not. More debt relative to equity creates more value from tax savings.

4. Because of the tax-deductibility of interest charges, WACC decreases as the amount of debt in the capital increases. WACC continues to decline until the costs associated with adding an additional dollar in debt (bankruptcy and agency) equal to benefits derived from the addition of debt (interest deductibility).

   Recall from Chapter 10: $k_e = E(R_i) = r_f + _i(R_m - r_f)$, and, $k_e = k_u$ $[1 + (D/E)]$ for a unique capital structure. Thus, increasing the weight of debt in the capital structure increases k_e, the required rate of return of equity holders (as equity holders are compensated for the added risk of their position corresponding to an increase of debt in the capital structure).

5. A. Project the firm's financing surplus or deficit: Project the free cash flows resulting from the proposed business plan as well as the financing cash flows resulting from the current capital structure.

   B. Set target credit rating and ratios: Determine the credit rating that the company wants to target in the future (given the need for additional funding, it is probably wise to maintain an investment-grade rating for better access to the capital markets).

C. Develop a capital structure for base case scenario: Identify and understand the key drivers of the financing deficit. Evaluate the familiar value drivers (growth and return on invested capital) to determine the uses and sources of free cash flow from operations (higher growth in general leads to greater cash requirements as investments in NPPE and working capital usually increase with growth; higher ROIC leads to lower cash requirements from higher operating margins over sales and a higher turnover of invested capital).

D. Test capital structure under downside scenario: Conduct a scenario analysis to analyze the impact of changes in key variables and how the changes might impact the financial risk of the firm.

E. Decide on current and future actions: Evaluate which elements of the financing plan need to be immediately implemented and which elements can be deferred to a later stage, when new information is available.

6. According to the pecking order theory, companies follow a specific pattern for acquiring the capital necessary to finance new projects. Companies meet their investment needs first by using internal funds (retained earnings), next by issuing debt, and finally by issuing shares of common stock.

   The pecking order hypothesis is premised in that actions undertaken by management provide a signal to the marketplace. Investors interpret the signals different financing alternatives represent as evidence of a company's financial prospects. For example, investors typically interpret an equity issue as a signal that management believes shares are overvalued. As a result managers turn to equity funding as a last resort because it could cause the share price to fall. According to the theory, companies tend to exhibit lower leverage when they are more mature and profitable, simply because they can fund internally and do not need any debt or equity funding.

18

Investor
Communications

1. A. A systematic approach helps executives communicate with investors more effectively and efficiently.

   B. A systematic approach can help align the market price of a company's shares with the company's intrinsic value. That alignment of share price and intrinsic value-and not simply the highest possible share price-should be the objective of investor relations.

2. A. A communication strategy grounded in a thoughtful analysis of market value relative to management's careful estimate of intrinsic value.

   B. An investment story that is consistent with the firm's underlying strategy and performance.

   C. Transparency about performance and the drivers of value (with some exceptions). Transparency includes providing operating measures that the company uses to run its business, as well as financial results.

3. The intrinsic value of a share of stock represents the present value of the future free cash flows provided by the firm discounted at the WACC. The market price of a share of stock is the equilibrium price of the last two market participants; what the demander of the common stock paid for the share and what the supplier of common stock received for the share.

   If the capital markets are perfectly efficient: Intrinsic value = Market price. As new information that impacts either future cash flows or risk an immediate and perfect price adjustment occurs. The less efficient the market, the longer the time interval between the new information entering the market and adjustment in market price.

4. Transparency in corporate communications are based on the free flow of publicly available information properly and fully identified, described adequately and accurately, and properly classified. Transparency guidelines should be consistently applied to parent and subsidiary, domestic and foreign subsidiary, affiliates and related entities over which the company has significant influence in order to prevent companies from the manipulating financial information.

5. Greater transparency is likely to cause tighter alignment between management's reasonable estimate of intrinsic value and the company's stock price. If investors better understand the drivers of historical and future performance, investors are able to develop more accurate models of the business. However, there is an important and valid argument against too much transparency: Disclosing too much may help a company's competitors, customers, and suppliers.

6. While the market is considered efficient in the long-term, short- and middle-term inefficiency in the market are frequently observed. Management is able to reduce these market inefficiencies by improving the alignment of company value to intrinsic value via systematic an approach to investor communication. Variances caused by inadequately met information needs and incomplete publicly available information can be offset by the greater transparency, information dissemination, explanation of corporate strategy, and an increased accuracy of forecasted value provided by an effective investor communications strategy.

19

Valuing Multibusiness Companies

1. A. Creating business unit financial statements.

   B. Estimating cost of capital for each business unit.

   C. Valuing each business separately, summing the parts, and interpreting the results.

2. A. Estimate each business unit's target capital structure. As a proxy for the target capital structure use the median capital structure of publicly traded peers, especially if most peers have similar capital structures.

   B. Next, using the debt levels based on industry medians, aggregate the business unit debt to see how the total compares with the company's total target debt. If the sum of business unit debt differs from the consolidated company's target debt record the difference as a corporate item, valuing its tax shield separately (or tax cost when the company is more conservatively financed). If the business unit has no comparable peers or if the capital structures of peers are widely different, allocate the consolidated debt across the business units so that each business unit has the same interest coverage ratio (EBITA/interest expense).

3. A pure top-down view of the firm will not highlight the disparity in value creation among individual business units within a company. Understanding that business units offer alternative avenues to value creation (differences in potential relative value of growth and margin improvement) provides a focus for managerial time and effort. Business unit valuation analysis also sets the stage for a comprehensive discussion of management priorities for operational improvement. Business unit

analysis, thus, provides striking insight into where value is being created or destroyed within the firm offering a road map for reorganizing the portfolio of businesses to maximize shareholder value.

4. In an efficient market a conglomerate discount should not exist, all firms should be properly valued based upon risk and cash flows received.

   Consensus has not been reached as to whether diversified firms are valued at a discount relative to a portfolio of pure plays in similar businesses. Among studies that claim a discount exists, there is no consensus about whether the discount results from the weaker performance of a diversified firm relative to a more focused firm, or whether the market values a diversified firm lower than a focused firm's peers because the company's business units had either lower growth or returns on capital relative to pure-play peers, thus, a performance discount versus a diversification/conglomerate discount.

5. A firms' target capital structure is a balancing act among company risk, free cash flows, and value. While we separate the investment decision (which assets and in what quantity to purchase) from the financing decision (what capital structure to employ) when determining a theoretically optimal capital structure in practice the separation is not so precise. A corporation's personality with respect to risk tolerance impacts both investment and financing decisions. The more conservative and risk adverse the company the greater both the investment in corporate assets and the degree of equity financing one observes. The more aggressive and risk tolerant the company the smaller both the investment in corporate assets and the degree of equity financing one observes.

   Total risk is comprised of operating risk (investment decisions) and financial risk (capital structure decisions). As detailed in Chapter 10, relevant risk may be proxied by beta that includes both operating (β_u) and financial risk components (β_L). Total risk may be managed by having one risk component being used to offset the other risk component. For example, too large a degree of operating risk can be offset by having a reduction of debt in the capital structure that in turn leads to a reduction in financial risk.

20

Valuing Flexibility

1. The decision rule for NPV is to accept a project when NPV is greater than or equal to 0. A NPV of 0 provides all the suppliers of the firm's capital their required rate of return.

2. A. Option to expand or contract.

   B. Option to extend or shorten.

   C. Option to increase or decrease scope.

   D. Option to switch.

3. A. Decision tree analysis.

   B. Real option valuation.

4. A. Estimate the standard NPV of the investment project without flexibility, using a traditional discounted cash flow model.

   B. Expand the DCF model into an event tree, mapping how the value of the project evolves over time, using unadjusted probabilities and the weighted average cost of capital.

   C. Turn the event tree into a decision tree by identifying the types of managerial flexibility that are available.

   D. Estimate the contingent NPV using a DTA or ROV approach.

5. A. The option to defer an investment decision.

   B. The option to abandon an investment decision.

6. Flexibility reduces the investment risk for this project, but the flexibility is essentially a call option on the project itself. By definition, call options are more risky per dollar invested than the underlying asset, and therefore require discounting their future cash flows at higher cost of capital. The total investment risk for the project with flexibility is lower because there is a much lower value exposed if the investment can be deferred. For the project including flexibility, a value of only $19.50 is at stake (with relatively high risk per dollar) whereas for the project without flexibility this amounts to $90.90 (with relatively low relative risk per dollar).

21

Cross-Border Valuation

1. When reorganizing a company's financial statements to estimate NOPLAT, invested capital and free cash according to the recommendations in Chapter 7, you will most often get similar results regardless of the accounting standards used to prepare the financial statements. For example, the way we treat goodwill and its amortization in NOPLAT and invested capital makes our concepts insensitive to whether companies actually amortize goodwill.

2. A. Language barriers.

   B. Different meanings of accounting terms.

   C. Different reporting frequencies and auditing standards.

   D. Inadequate disclosure.

3. A. In one year, GBP/USD is expected to be 0.66312.

   B. Thus, USD equivalent earned is GBP 0.71352/GBP/USD 0.66312 or 1.076.

   C. Your conclusion about risk-free rates across heavily arbitraged currency borders is that it does not seem to matter what risk-free rate you use for cost of capital calculations in well-arbitraged markets.

4. A. What are the relevant tax rates and taxable income?

   B. Can fiscal grouping be applied to offset profits and losses of different entities?

   C. What are the relevant cross-border taxation issues?

   D. How does taxation affect shareholders in different countries?

5. The interest rate parity formula states that:

$$X_t = X_0 + \frac{1 + r_f}{1 + r_d}$$

$$X_t = 1.53_0 + \frac{1 + .0225_f}{1 + .015_d} = 1.541 \text{ USD}$$

6.

Inventory, this year = 6,320,000 Euro $0.87 = \$ \ 5,498,400$

Inventory, last year = 6,320,000 Euro $1.15 = \$ \ 7,268,000$

Loss = ($1,779,000)

22

Valuation in Emerging Markets

1. A. Assets and liabilities are recorded at historical cost and not revalued to current levels of currency units.

   B. Nominal year-to-year comparisons and ratio analysis become meaningless (e.g., ROIC and PP&E/Revenue).

   C. Continuing value cash flows require growth and expected returns to reflect highly variable economic conditions.

2. A. Ensure that the WACC estimates in real terms (WACCR) and nominal terms (WACCN) are defined consistently with the inflation assumptions in each year.

   B. The value-driver formula as presented in Chapter 9 should be adjusted when estimating continuing value in real terms. The returns on capital in real-terms projections overestimate the economic returns in the case of positive net working capital. The free cash flow in real terms differs from the cash flow implied by the value driver formula by an amount equal to the annual monetary loss on net working capital.

   C. When using the continuing-value formulas, make sure the explicit forecast period is long enough for the model to reach a steady state with constant growth rates of free cash flow.

3. A. Real forecasts make it impossible to calculate taxes correctly and easily lead to errors in calculating working capital changes; companies grow in real terms when operating efficiencies improve.

   B. The main downside of using nominal cash flows is that future capital expenditures are difficult to project because the typically stable relationship between revenues and fixed assets does not hold under high inflation. As a result, depreciation charges also are difficult to project.

4. A. Forecast operating performance in real terms.

   B. Build financial statements in nominal terms.

   C. Build financial statements in real terms.

   D. Forecast the future free cash flows in real and nominal terms from the projected income statements and balance sheets.

   E. Estimate DCF value in real and nominal terms.

5. A. Growth is overstated in times of high inflation, thus, restate in real terms.

   B. Capital turnover is generally overstated because operating assets are carried at historical costs, thus restate value with inflation index.

   C. Operating margins may be overstated because of too low depreciation and large gains on slow-moving inventory.

   D. Credit, market, debt, and activity ratios may be distorted because long-term assets are understated relative to replacement costs and floating debt is at current currency units.

6. Here is a solution of the comparison of the various techniques:

   A. Unadjusted deflated projections:

Proforma Financials	Unadjusted Deflated Forecasts				Continuing Value
	1	2	3	4	15
Revenues	$1,000	$1,050	$1,103	$1,158	$1,292
EBITDA	300	315	331	347	387
Depreciation	(70)	(80)	(84)	(88)	(102)
Operating income	230	235	247	259	285
Tax	(115)	(118)	(123)	(130)	(143)
NOPLAT	$ 115	$ 118	$ 123	$ 130	$ 143
Working capital	$ 200	$ 210	$ 221	$ 232	$ 258
NPPE (begin of year)	350	400	420	441	511
Less: Depreciation	(70)	(80)	(84)	(88)	(102)
Plus: Capex	120	100	105	110	107
Net PPE (end of year)	400	420	441	463	517
Invested capital	$ 600	$ 630	$ 662	$ 695	$ 775
EBITDA		$ 315	$ 331	$ 347	$ 387
Less: Tax		(118)	(123)	(130)	(143)
Less: Capex		(100)	(105)	(110)	(107)
Less: Working capital increase		(10)	(11)	(11)	(3)
Free cash flow		$ 88	$ 92	$ 96	$ 135

B. Nominal projections—note that Capex projections are derived from underlying real projections for revenues and capital turnover:

Proforma Financials	Nominal Forecasts				Continuing Value
	1	2	3	4	15
Revenues	$1,000	$1,575	$1,985	$2,292	$4,374
EBITDA	300	473	595	688	1,312
Depreciation	(70)	(80)	(94)	(113)	(277)
Operating income	230	393	501	575	1,035
Tax	(115)	(196)	(251)	(287)	(518)
NOPLAT	$ 115	$ 196	$ 251	$ 287	$ 518
Working capital	$ 200	$ 315	$ 397	$ 458	$ 875
NPPE (begin of year)	350	400	470	565	1,385
Less: Depreciation	(70)	(80)	(94)	(113)	(277)
Plus: Capex	120	150	189	218	364
Net PPE (end of year)	400	470	565	670	1,472
Invested capital	$ 600	$ 785	$ 962	$1,129	$2,347
EBITDA		$ 473	$ 595	$ 688	$1,312
Less: Tax		(196)	251	(287)	(518)
Less: Capex		(150)	(189)	(218)	(364)
Less: Working capital increase		(115)	(82)	(62)	(50)
Free cash flow		$ 11	$ 74	$ 121	$ 381

C. Real projections—note that real tax projections are based on nominal tax projections:

| Proforma Financials | Real Forecasts | | | | Continuing Value |
	1	2	3	4	15
Revenues	$1,000	$1,050	$1,103	$1,158	$1,292
EBITDA	300	315	331	347	387
Depreciation	(70)	(80)	(84)	(88)	(102)
Operating income	230	235	247	259	285
Tax	(115)	(131)	(139)	(145)	(153)
NOPLAT	$ 115	$ 104	$ 107	$ 114	$ 132
Working capital	$ 200	$ 210	$ 221	$ 232	$ 258
NPPE (begin of year)	350	400	420	441	511
Less: Depreciation	(70)	(80)	(84)	(88)	(102)
Plus: Capex	120	100	105	110	107
Net PPE (end of year)	400	420	441	463	517
Invested capital	$ 600	$ 630	$ 662	$ 695	$ 775
EBITDA		$ 315	$ 331	$ 347	$ 387
Less: Tax		(131)	(139)	(145)	(153)
Less: Capex		(100)	(105)	(110)	(107)
Less: Working capital monetary result and increase		(77)	(46)	(31)	(15)
Free cash flow		$ 7	$ 41	$ 61	$ 112

D. Comparison—note that real free cash is identical for nominal and real forecasts:

	Forecasts				Continuing Value
Unadjusted Deflated	**1**	**2**	**3**	**4**	**15**
Real NOPLAT	115	118	123	130	143
Real free cash flow		88	92	96	135
Invested capital/revenue	0.60	0.60	0.60	0.60	0.60
ROIC pretax	38%	37%	37%	37%	37%
ROIC posttax	19%	19%	19%	19%	18%
Nominal					
Real NOPLAT*	115	131	139	145	153
Real free cash flow*		7	41	61	112
Invested capital/revenue	0.60	0.50	0.48	0.49	0.54
ROIC pretax	38%	50%	52%	51%	44%
ROIC posttax	19%	25%	26%	25%	22%
Real					
Real NOPLAT*	115	104	107	114	132
Real free cash flow*		7	41	61	112
Invested capital/revenue	0.60	0.60	0.60	0.60	0.60
ROIC pretax	38%	37%	37%	37%	37%
ROIC posttax	19%	17%	16%	16%	17%

*Deflated NOPLAT and free cash at inflation index.

7. Discounted cash flow with inflation and real growth effects:

A. Nominal WACC = $(1 + \text{Real WACC}) \times (1 + \text{Inflation rate}) - 1 = 1.08 \times 1.05 - 1 = 13$ percent

B. Nominal growth rate = $(1 + \text{Real growth}) \times (1 + \text{Inflation}) - 1 = 1.01 \times 1.05 - 1 = 6$ percent

C. Unadjusted deflated DCF:

Results		Forecasts				Continuing Value
	1	2	3	4	5–14	15
Real WACC	8%	8%	8%	8%		8%
Unadjusted deflated free cash flow		88	92	96		135
Continuing value						1,947
Discount factor		0.926	0.857	0.794		0.340
PV of free cash flow		81	79	77	676	709
Unadjusted deflated DCF	1,621					

D. Nominal DCF:

Results		Forecasts				Continuing Value
	1	2	3	4	5–14	15
Nominal WACC	30%	62%	30%	19%		13%
Nominal free cash flow		11	74	121		381
Continuing value						5,559
Discount factor		0.617	0.476	0.401		0.101
PV of free cash flow		7	35	48	553	597
Nominal DCF	1,241					

E. Real DCF:

Results	Forecasts 1	2	3	4	5–14	Continuing Value 15
Real WACC	8%	8%	8%	8%		8%
Real free cash flow		7	41	61		112
Continuing value						1,641
Discount factor		0.926	0.857	0.794		0.340
PV of free cash flow		7	35	48	553	597
Real DCF	1,241					

F. Comment on the results:

Nominal and real cash flow projections can both generate the right answer for the DCF value, but neither approach is perfect.

When projecting cash flows in real terms, you cannot calculate taxes correctly because taxes are based on nominal profits. Furthermore, the investment in working capital does not automatically follow from the annual change in working capital. Therefore, project real taxes and real investments in working capital by deflating the nominal projections for these items.

Projecting cash flows in nominal terms is difficult because future capital expenditures are difficult to estimate. The relationship between revenues and fixed assets changes over time under high inflation. As a result, depreciation charges also are difficult to project. Therefore, project nominal capital expenditures by inflating the capital expenditures from real forecasts. Nominal projections for net PPE are then derived from net PPE at begin of year plus capital expenditures minus depreciation.

Never project cash flows by simply deflating forecasts of revenues without any of the adjustments to real cash flows as described above: This leads to the wrong DCF value (compare unadjusted deflated DCF to real and nominal DCF).

23

Valuing High-Growth Companies

1. In the valuation of an established company, the first step is to analyze historical performance. But in the case of a high-growth company, historical financial results provide limited clues about future prospects. Therefore, for a high-growth firm begin with the future, not with the past. The future state should be defined and bounded by measures of operating performance, such as penetration rates, average revenue per customer, and sustainable gross margins. Focus on sizing the future market, predicting the level of profitability, and estimating the investments necessary to achieve success. To do this, choose a point well into the future, at a time when financial performance is likely to stabilize, and begin forecasting.

   In the case of a new chief executive office at the helm of a corporation, the historic approach to managing the business may be replaced by a new strategy. If significant changes in the processes employed to manage a firm's resources take place, a review of historic performance provides little guidance for future prospects. In this case, a more detailed forecast of future opportunities and performance provides better value estimates.

2. A probability-weighted scenario can highlight the economic issues driving a company's value. Using just a few scenarios makes critical assumptions and interactions more transparent than other modeling approaches. One can use scenario analysis to determine the value impact of changes in individual drivers.

3. Focus on sizing the future market, predicting the level of profitability, and estimating the investments necessary to achieve success. To do this, choose a point well into the future at a time when financial performance is likely to stabilize, and begin forecasting. Work backward to link it to current performance. Measures of current performance are likely to commingle investments and expenses, so when possible, capitalize hidden investments (even those expensed under traditional accounting rules). Do not rely on a single long-term forecast. Describe the market's development in terms of multiple scenarios including total size, ease of competitive entry, and so on. When you build a comprehensive scenario, be sure all forecasts, including revenue growth, profitability margins, and required investment, are consistent with the underlying assumptions of the particular scenario. Finally, apply probabilistic weights to each scenario. The weights must be consistent with long-term historical evidence on corporate growth.

4.

Area	B2C	B2B
Drivers	Market penetration, customer churn rates, cost per customer/channel	Efficiency of service, segmentation of procurement channels, cost per channel, technology diffusion rates
Controlling growth	Call center tracking with market, fulfillment standards, profit per customer	Straight-through processing across multiple activities, standardized contracting, market feed back mechanisms
Scenarios	Customer segmentation basis	Product and services segmentation basis

24

Valuing Cyclical Companies

1. A. Base years will either be too high or too low as a basis for forecasting future cash flows.

   B. Share prices reflect high levels of volatility.

2. A. Use past cycles to value the normal-cycle scenario.

   B. Use recent performance to construct a new-trend-line scenario.

   C. Consider supply and demand growth, new entries and exits from the industry, technology, and government changes as the rationale for the two scenarios.

   D. Assign probabilities to each scenario and calculate expected value.

3. A. Two scenarios are produced: a normal scenario that will be defined (naively!) as the average scenario over the past five years and a new-trend scenario that will reflect both industry and GP recent activity.

   The normal scenario is produced from the following data: Following the assumptions of average starting asset and sales, as well as average ratios and zero growth. One possible normal scenario produces this valuation.

   The normal scenario produces a stock price of $35.10 within the five-year range of about $23 to $54 GP experienced between 2001 and 2005. A key driver of this average scenario is that ROIC exceeds the cost of capital in each forecast year and in perpetuity.

	2001	2002	2003	2004	2005
Invested capital statement					
Working capital	831	125	(104)	(3)	368
Long term assets	9,740	10,203	10,034	10,055	12,338
Operating invested capital	10,571	10,328	9,930	10,052	12,706
Net investment		(243)	(398)	122	2,654
Debt	7,052	6,817	6,460	6,928	8,831
Equity	3,519	3,511	3,470	3,124	3,875
					22.50
NOPLAT statement					
Sales	14,313	13,024	13,094	13,342	17,977
Operating expenses	(9,794)	(9,798)	(10,209)	(10,231)	(13,333)
General expenses	(1,406)	(1,475)	(1,296)	(1,204)	(1,670)
Depreciation	(984)	(996)	(1,017)	(997)	(1,013)
EBIT	2,129	755	572	910	1,961
Taxes on EBIT	(852)	(350)	(346)	(386)	(759)
Change in deferred taxes	10	14	100	38	73
NOPLAT	1,287	419	326	562	1,275
Provision for income taxes	679	135	106	202	705
Tax shield on interest expense	173	213	282	188	192
Tax on investment income	—	—	(78)	(10)	(137)
Tax on non-operating income	—	2	36	6	—
Taxes on EBIT	852	350	346	386	759
Net income statement					
Sales	14,313	13,024	13,094	13,342	17,977
Operating expenses	(9,794)	(9,798)	(10,209)	(10,231)	(13,333)
General expenses	(1,406)	(1,475)	(1,296)	(1,204)	(1,670)
Depreciation	(984)	(996)	(1,017)	(997)	(1,013)
EBIT	2,129	755	572	910	1,961
Investment income	—	—	128	24	355
Investment expense	(432)	(459)	(465)	(443)	(495)
Miscellaneous, net	—	(5)	(60)	(15)	—
Earnings before taxes	1,697	291	175	476	1,821
Income taxes	(679)	(135)	(106)	(202)	(705)
Net income (before extra items)	1,018	156	69	274	1,116
Tax rate	−40%	−46%	−61%	−42%	−39%

	2001	2002	2003	2004	2005
Reconciliation to net income statement					
Net income	1,018	156	69	274	1,116
Add: increase in deferred taxes	10	14	100	38	73
Adjusted net income	1,028	170	169	312	1,189
Add: Interest expense after tax	259	246	183	255	303
Income available to investors	1,287	416	352	567	1,492
Less: Interest income after tax	—	—	(50)	(14)	(218)
Less: Non-operating income after tax	—	3	24	9	—
NOPLAT	1,287	419	326	562	1,275
ROIC tree					
ROIC		4.0%	3.2%	5.7%	12.7%
= (1 − EBIT cash tax rate)		55.5%	56.9%	61.7%	65.0%
× Pretax ROIC		7.1%	5.5%	9.2%	19.5%
= EBIT/Sales		5.8%	4.4%	6.8%	10.9%
× Sales/Invested capital		1.23	1.27	1.34	1.79
EBIT/Sales					
= 1 − (Operating expenses/Sales		75.2%	78.0%	76.7%	74.2%
+ General expenses/Sales		11.3%	9.9%	9.0%	9.3%
+ Depreciation/Sales)		7.6%	7.8%	7.5%	5.6%
Sales/Invested capital = 1 /(Operating working capital/Sales		6.4%	1.0%	−0.8%	0.0%
+ Long term operating assets/Sales)		74.8%	77.9%	75.2%	55.9%
Change in deferred tax/Sales		0.107%	0.764%	0.285%	0.406%
Free cash flow statement					
NOPLAT		419	326	562	1,275
Depreciation		996	1,017	997	1,013
Gross cash flow		1,415	1,343	1,559	2,288

(continued)

	2001	2002	2003	2004	2005
Increase in operating working capital		(706)	(229)	101	371
Capital expenditures		1,459	848	1,018	3,296
Gross investment		753	619	1,119	3,667
Free cash flow		662	724	440	(1,379)
Non-operating cash flow		(5)	68	9	355
Cash flow available to investors		657	792	449	(1,024)
Cost of capital					
Beta		1.33	1.33	1.33	1.33
Debt/invested capital		66.7%	66.0%	65.1%	68.9%
Equity/invested capital		33.3%	34.0%	34.9%	31.1%
Cost of debt		6.5%	6.8%	6.9%	7.1%
Cost of equity		15.0%	15.0%	15.0%	15.0%
Weighted average cost of capital		7.3%	6.9%	7.8%	7.7%
Economic profit					
NOPLAT		418.7	325.5	561.8	1,274.8
Capital charge		(772.8)	(708.9)	(774.4)	(771.0)
Economic profit		(354.0)	(383.3)	(212.6)	503.8

	Average 2001–2005	F 2006	F 2007	F 2008	CV 2009
Working capital	243,400	254,752	266,634	279,070	—
Net fixed assets	10,474,000	10,962,507	11,473,798	12,008,935	—
Invested capital	10,717,400	11,217,259	11,740,431	12,288,005	12,861,117
Net investment		499,859	523,172	547,573	573,112
Debt	7,217,600	7,554,229	7,906,557	8,275,319	8,661,279
Equity	3,499,800	3,663,031	3,833,874	4,012,686	4,199,837
Sales growth		4.66%	4.66%	4.66%	
Net sales	14,350,000	15,019,283	15,719,782	16,452,952	
Operating expense		(11,170,788)	(11,691,793)	(12,237,098)	
General expense		(1,475,972)	(1,544,811)	(1,616,861)	
Depreciation		(1,048,105)	(1,096,989)	(1,148,152)	
EBIT		1,324,418	1,386,189	1,450,841	
Taxes on EBIT		(512,748)	(536,663)	(561,693)	
Change in deferred tax		58,654	61,389	64,253	
Net operating profit less adjusted tax		870,324	910,915	953,400	997,867
Net investment		(499,859)	(523,172)	(547,573)	(573,112)
Free cash flow		370,465	387,743	405,827	424,755
Cost of capital		7.46%	7.46%	7.46%	7.46%
Economic profit		70,822	74,125	77,582	81,201
Beta	1.37	1.368	1.368	1.368	1.368
Unlevered beta	0.6043	0.5827	0.5827	0.5827	0.5827
PV factors	1	0.930580162	0.865979439	0.805863287	

	Average 2001–2005	F 2006	F 2007	F 2008	CV 2009
	PV sums				
PV short term forecast	1,007,566	344,747	335,777	327,041	
Continuing value				15,192,342	
PV continuing value	12,242,951				
Market value of asset	13,250,516				
Debt	(7,217,600)				
Market value of equity	6,032,916				
Number of shares	172.3				
Stock price	35.01				
	Sum				
PV economic profit 1–3	192,617	65,906	64,191	62,521	
Continuing value				2,904,337	
PV continuing value	2,340,499				
Invested capital	10,717,400				
Market value of asset	13,250,516				
ROIC	6.36%	8.12%	8.12%	8.12%	8.12%
D/IC	67.34%	67.34%	67.34%	67.34%	67.34%
Eq/IC	32.66%	32.66%	32.66%	32.66%	32.66%
Tax rate	38.71%	38.71%	38.71%	38.71%	38.71%
Interest rate	6.83%	6.83%	6.83%	6.83%	6.83%
Growth (investment/ capital)		4.66%	4.66%	4.66%	4.66%
Investment rate (Gwh/ROIC)		57.43%	57.43%	57.43%	57.43%
EBIT/sales		8.8181%	8.8181%	8.8181%	
Sales/IC		1.4014	1.4014	1.4014	
WC/sales	1.6962%	1.6962%	1.6962%	1.6962%	
NFAOA/sales	72.9895%	72.9895%	72.9895%	72.9895%	
Operating expenses/sales	74.3763%	74.3763%	74.3763%	74.3763%	74.3763%
SG&A/sales	9.8272%	9.8272%	9.8272%	9.8272%	9.8272%
Deprecation/sales	6.9784%	6.9784%	6.9784%	6.9784%	6.9784%
Change in deferred tax/sales	0.391%	0.391%	0.391%	0.391%	0.391%

B. A new trend can be established from industry growth trends. For example, based on recent industry growth and GP's recent plans to attain and exceed industry efficiency, profitability, and growth standards, the following new-trend scenario assumptions can be made: Sales growth (5-year) 6 percent; Beta 1.01; Operating expense/sales 70 percent. To attain 10.20 percent EBIT/sales, operating expenses must be no more than 73 percent of sales.

A financial engineering overhaul of debt-equity and pumped up investor relations may have little or no effect on beta in the cyclical paper and pulp industry, and thus, keep current beta levels at about 1.37. This also encourages managers to achieve higher shareholder return expectations and take more risks controlled by realized results.

Maintain long-run 4.66 percent sales growth. Increase near-term sales growth to 8 percent.

Value the new-trend scenario using the following templates:

	Average 2001–2005	F 2006	F 2007	F 2008	CV 2009
Working capital	243,400	258,004	273,484	289,893	—
Net fixed assets	10,474,000	11,102,440	11,768,586	12,474,702	—
Invested capital	10,717,400	11,360,444	12,042,071	12,764,595	13,359,935
Net investment		643,044	681,627	722,524	595,340
Debt	7,217,600	7,650,656	8,109,695	8,596,277	8,997,207
Equity	3,499,800	3,709,788	3,932,375	4,168,318	4,362,728
Sales growth		6.00%	6.00%	6.00%	
Net sales	14,350,000	15,211,000	16,123,660	17,091,080	
Operating expense		(11,104,030)	(11,770,272)	(12,476,488)	
General expense		(1,494,812)	(1,584,501)	(1,679,571)	
Depreciation		(1,061,484)	(1,125,173)	(1,192,683)	
EBIT		1,550,674	1,643,714	1,742,337	
Taxes on EBIT		(600,343)	(636,364)	(674,546)	
Change in deferred tax		59,402	62,967	66,745	
Net operating profit less adjusted tax		1,009,733	1,070,317	1,134,536	1,187,451
Net investment		(643,044)	(681,627)	(722,524)	(595,340)
Free cash flow		366,689	388,690	412,012	592,111
Cost of capital		7.46%	7.46%	7.46%	7.46%
Economic profit		210,232	222,846	236,216	235,232
Beta	1.37	1.368	1.368	1.368	1.368
Unlevered beta	0.6043	0.5827	0.5827	0.5827	0.5827
PV factors	1	0.930580162	0.865979439	0.805863287	
	PV sums				
PV short term forecast	1,009,857	341,234	336,598	332,025	
Continuing value				21,178,205	
PV continuing value	17,066,738				
Market value of asset	18,076,594				
Debt	(7,217,600)				
Market value of equity	10,858,994				
Number of shares	172.3				
Stock price	63.02				

(continued)

	Average 2001–2005	F 2006	F 2007	F 2008	CV 2009
	Sum				
PV economic profit 1–3	578,975	195,637	192,980	190,358	
Continuing value				8,413,610	
PV continuing value	6,780,219				
Invested capital	10,717,400				
Market value of asset	18,076,594				
ROIC	6.36%	9.42%	9.42%	9.42%	9.30%
D/IC	67.34%	67.34%	67.34%	67.34%	67.34%
Eq/IC	32.66%	32.66%	32.66%	32.66%	32.66%
Tax rate	38.71%	38.71%	38.71%	38.71%	38.71%
Interest rate	6.83%	6.83%	6.83%	6.83%	6.83%
Growth (Investment/ Capital)		6.00%	6.00%	6.00%	4.66%
Investment rate (Growth/ROIC)		63.68%	63.68%	63.68%	50.14%
EBIT/Sales		10.1944%	10.1944%	10.1944%	
Sales/IC		1.4193	1.4193	1.4193	
WC/Sales	1.6962%	1.6962%	1.6962%	1.6962%	
NFAOA/Sales	72.9895%	72.9895%	72.9895%	72.9895%	
Operating expenses/Sales	74.3763%	73.0000%	73.0000%	73.0000%	73.0000%
SG&A/Sales	9.8272%	9.8272%	9.8272%	9.8272%	9.8272%
Deprecation/Sales	6.9784%	6.9784%	6.9784%	6.9784%	6.9784%
Change in deferred tax/Sales	0.391%	0.391%	0.391%	0.391%	0.391%

These assumptions will result in a $63.20 share price, not quite double the normal scenario value. analysis can be performed to justify each of the scenarios.

C. The analysis can be performed to justify each of the scenarios.

D. If the normal scenario occurs 70 percent of the time (based on IBES earnings forecast variations) and the new trend scenario occurs 30 percent of the time, then the stock price is about $45 per share.

Scenario	Probability (%)	Value
Normal	70	35
New trend	30	63

25

Valuing Financial Institutions

A. Calculate net income with the income model:

Interest income	$93.5
Interest expense	(38.0)
Other expenses	(40.0)
Net profit before taxes	15.5
Taxes	(6.2)
Net income	$9.3

B. Calculate net income with the spread model:

Loan spread	$34.0
Deposit spread	28.5
Equity spread	3.5
Reserve debt	(10.5)
Expenses	(40.0)
Net profit before taxes	15.5
Taxes	(6.2)
Net income	$9.3

C. The two approaches are equivalent, as the numerical example shows. Here's an algebraic demonstration according to the income model:

$$NI = (r_L L - r_D D - E)(1 - T)$$

where r_L and r_D are the loan and deposit rates, E is the noninterest expense and T is the marginal tax rate.

For the spread model:

$$NI = [(r_L - r_M)L + (r_M - r_D)D + r_M S - r_M D - E](1 - T)$$

where r_M = the money rate of return.

The equivalence between the two approaches can be viewed by way of the balance sheet relation:

$$R + L = D + S$$

or

$$D + S - R - L = 0$$

where R = Cash reserve
      L = Loans
      D = Deposits
      S = Equity

Gathering the terms in r_M in the spread model we have:

$$NI = [r_L L - r_D D + r_M(D + S - R - L) - E](1 - T)$$
$$= [r_L L - r_D D - E](1 - T)$$

Just the same as the income model from the financial statements. In constructing the spread model, banks use an assumed yield, the money rate, to benchmark the profitability of loans and deposits and debit the lack of earning ability of cash reserves at the Fed. To square the earning abilities of various parts of the balance sheet with net income, the same rate must be used as a proxy for the cost of equity capital. The problem lies in the use of this rate to benchmark loans and deposits, and to cost the equity. Each of these items has a different risk-adjusted cost of capital, and thus a different benchmark. Certainly the money rate is not at all necessarily related to the equity cost of capital and can be reliably assigned only to the cash reserve account. Allocations based on the spread model must be viewed with caution since they do not represent comparisons of investments (short and long) with their risk-adjusted opportunity costs of capital.

2. The model starts with a forecast of *deposit* growth. Loans are then determined by a *loan to total asset* ratio. *Cash* reserves work from a cash reserve-to-total deposit ratio, reflecting Federal Reserve policy. Premises, equipment, and other assets are required to support deposits directly and loans indirectly. Investments are related to cash reserves. Given a level of *deposit derived total assets,* a managerially determined *liability* to total asset relationship is determined. Federal Funds purchased balances_*liabilities. Equity* balances the balance sheet. Noninterest income and expense are related to deposit size. Forecasts of interest rates drive the *deposits,* term borrowing, investment, and *loan* rates.

3. A. Calculate net income using the template on page 182.

   B. Calculate the balance sheet using the template on page 183.

   C. Calculate equity cash flows and the value to equity holders using template on page 184.

Income Statement

| | Explicit Forecast Period | | | | | | | | CV Period | |
| | 2005 | | 2006 | | 2007 | | 2008 | | 2009 | |
	Amount	Rate (%)	Amount	Rate (%)	Amount	Rate (%)	Amount	Rate (%)	Amount	Rate (%)
Interest income	66.919	8.11	87.087	8.89	104.880	9.63	123.306	10.37	83.527	7.08
Less: interest expense	(25.221)	3.52	(33.501)	3.91	(45.286)	4.76	(58.346)	5.62	(46.686)	4.59
Net interest income	41.698	4.59	53.587	4.97	59.594	4.87	64.960	4.75	36.841	2.49
Plus: other income	5.120		5.619		6.293		6.923		6.923	
Less: other expenses	(26.498)		(30.717)		(34.403)		(37.844)		(37.844)	
Net profit before tax	20.320		82.075		91.077		98.999		42.761	
Less: taxes	(7.721)	38.00	(31.188)	38.00	(34.609)	38.00	(37.620)	38.00	(16.249)	38.00
Net income	12.598		50.886		56.468		61.379		26.512	

Balance Sheet

| | Explicit Forecast Period | | | | | | | | CV Period | |
| | 2005 | | 2006 | | 2007 | | 2008 | | 2009 | |
	Amount	Rate (%)	Amount	Rate (%)	Amount	Rate (%)	Amount	Rate (%)	Amount	Rate (%)
Cash reserves	32.411		37.460		41.955		46.151		46.151	
Investment Securities	378.520	6.93	440.706	7.68	493.591	8.43	542.950	9.18	542.950	6.00
Net loans	446.135	9.12	539.425	9.87	595.765	10.62	646.111	11.37	636.881	8.00
Net premises, other assets	25.526		29.369		32.893		36.182		36.182	
Less: provision for credit losses	(6.281)		(7.552)		(8.341)		(9.046)		(8.916)	
Total assets	876.311		1,039.408		1,155.863		1,262.349		1,253.248	
Interest bearing deposits	552.892	3.29	635.826	4.29	712.125	5.29	783.337	6.29	783.337	5.00
Non-interest-bearing deposits	98.587		113.375		126.980		139.678		139.678	
Other short-term liabilities	6.102		7.276		8.091		8.836		8.773	
Federal funds purchased	57.300	4.00	95.838		100.612		103.274		83.342	
Term borrowings	105.550	4.49	124.729	4.99	138.704	5.49	151.482	5.99	150.390	5.00
Liabilities	820.431		977.043		1,086.511		1,186.608		1,165.520	
Shareholders' equity	55.880	13.48	62.364	14.02	69.352	14.56	75.741	14.56	87.727	14.02
Total	876.311		1,039.408		1,155.863		1,262.349		1,253.248	

Equity Cash Flow and Value

| | 2005 | Explicit Forecast Period | | | CV Period |
		2006	2007	2008	2009
Net income		50.886	56.468	61.379	26.512
Less: increase in assets		(163.097)	(116.455)	(106.485)	9.101
Plus: increase in liabilities		156.612	109.468	100.096	(21.087)
Equity cash flow					
Present value factor		0.8770391	0.7655719	0.6682715	
PV equity cash flows					
PV continuing value					
Market value of equity					
Per number of shares	5.987				
Stock price					

4.

Value Drivers	
Industrial Companies	**Financial Companies**
A. Growth	A. Growth
B. Return on capital (relative to the cost of capital)	B. Return on equity

5. Duration is a measure of flow time to cash defined as the present value cash flow-weighted average of the times to the receipt of the cash flows. Thus, duration is a valuable model defining the average maturity of the assets and liabilities of the financial institution. Modifying duration, by adjusting for market interest rates, provides a proxy of interest rate sensitivity of any asset or liability. Thus, duration is the critical model used to immunize assets and liabilities from interest rate changes. Finally, duration is a useful model to estimate an assets change in value given a change in market interest rates.

6. Reserves represent the present value of expected benefits and claims to be paid out (less the present value of expected premiums for life insurers). Insurers use actuarial guidelines to estimate the size of reserves, taking into account such factors as underlying customer risks, persistence (rate of renewals), investment returns, and inflation. The life insurance company's reserve position similar to a company's accumulated pension obligation in that both represent an estimated present value of future contractual cash outflow obligations.

MASTER

VALUATION

WITH THESE NEW RESOURCES FROM JOHN WILEY & SONS

Valuation

0-471-70218-8 • cloth • 768 pages • $85.00

- Includes in-depth coverage of real options and insurance companies, along with detailed instructions on how to drive value creation, and expert advice on how to manage difficult situations.

- Fully updated and expanded to reflect business conditions in today's volatile global economy.

- Contains detailed case studies showing how various techniques and principles can be applied in the real world.

Fourth Edition

Completely Updated! Over 350,000 Copies Sold

VALUATION

MEASURING
and MANAGING
the VALUE
of COMPANIES

TIM KOLLER · MARC GOEDHART · DAVID WESSELS

McKINSEY & COMPANY

Valuation Spreadsheet

Available via download or on CD-ROM at **WileyValuation.com**

Download • 0-471-73389-X • 272 pages • $150.00
CD-ROM • 0-471-70217-X • $150.00

- This easy-to-use interactive tool gives users a practical application of concepts learned in *Valuation, Fourth Edition.*

- Spreadsheets help compute a company's valuation based on the user's inputs.

- Available in Excel.

TWO EASY WAYS TO ORDER:

- Call 1-877-762-2974
- Visit us at WileyValuation.com

WileyValuation.com

Building off of the success of *Valuation*—the #1 guide to corporate valuation from the international management-consulting firm McKinsey & Company—**WileyValuation.com** is the premier destination Web site for institutional investors, corporate finance professionals, and academics.

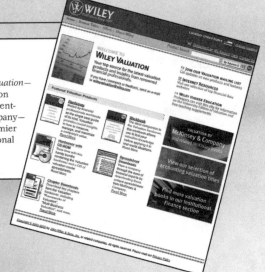

WILEY

Now you know.

wiley.com